Praise

FATHERING RIGHT

"Dr. Heinowitz hits the target immediately by exclaiming, 'You're both pregnant.' When he follows up with tips on facing fears, becoming a wiser lover, and fathering forever, we're hooked. *Fathering Right from the Start* offers a definitive map for fathering success through involvement. Read it whenever you can—before, during, or after pregnancy."

—Alan Thicke
Actor (star of TV's *Growing Pains*), producer,
and author of *How Men Have Babies*

"If fatherhood seems like Mount Everest to you, here is your guide. Jack Heinowitz will get you safely and happily to the top."

—David B. Chamberlain, Ph.D.
Author of *The Mind of Your Newborn Baby*

"Jack Heinowitz speaks to fathers with compassion and understanding. *Fathering Right from the Start* provides truly helpful information about the deeper issues of fatherhood and gives dads real tools for getting through the tough times."

—Peggy O'Mara
Editor and publisher, *Mothering* Magazine

"*Fathering Right from the Start* presents fathers with a heartwarming concept of their importance in the lives of their infants and children. Dr. Heinowitz not only enlightens us about the role of a father but also provides unique insights and exercises to help guide men in improving their performance both as dads and as partners. This book is a must-read for all new and experienced fathers."

—Marshall Klaus, M.D., pediatrician, researcher
—Phyllis Klaus, M.F.T., C.S.W., psychotherapist, family therapist
Coauthors of *Bonding, Mothering the Mother,* and
Your Amazing Newborn

Fathering

RIGHT FROM THE START

Also by Jack Heinowitz:

The *Pregnant Fathers* Series

> *Pregnant Fathers: How Fathers Can Enjoy and Share the Experiences of Pregnancy and Childbirth*
> (Prentice Hall Press, 1982)

> *Pregnant Fathers: Entering Parenthood Together*
> (Parents As Partners Press, 1995)

> *Pregnant Fathers: Becoming the Father You Want to Be*
> (Andrews and McMeel, 1997)

Fathering

RIGHT FROM THE START

Straight Talk about Pregnancy, Birth, and Beyond

JACK HEINOWITZ, PH.D.

Foreword by Wade F. Horn, Ph.D.
President of The National Fatherhood Initiative

NEW WORLD LIBRARY
NOVATO, CALIFORNIA

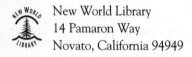 New World Library
14 Pamaron Way
Novato, California 94949

Editor: Ellen Kleiner
Interior design: Janice St. Marie
Copyright © 2001 by Jack Heinowitz

Library of Congress Cataloging-in-Publication Data
Heinowitz. Jack.
    Fathering right from the start : straight talk about
pregnancy, birth, and beyond / Jack Heinowitz. — 1st
ed.
        p. cm.
    Includes bibliographical references.
    Preassigned LCCN: 99-70364
    ISBN 1-57731-187-6
    1. Pregnancy. 2. Father and child. 3. Pregnancy—
Psychological aspects. 4. Childbirth. 5. Parenting.
    6. Fathers. I. Title.
RG525.H42 1999   618.2'4
QBI99-900439

First printing, April 2001
ISBN 1-57731-187-6
Printed in Canada on acid-free, recycled paper
Distributed to the trade by Publishers Group West

10 9 8 7 6 5 4 3 2

To Harold, my dad, my compass and companion;
Jesse, my son, my fountain of inspiration and beaming beacon;
and Ellen, my life partner and sustainer of my soul.

Contents

Acknowledgments

To the best support and birthing team a middle-aged father could ever hope for—Ellen Kleiner, one and only; Bob Goodman; Janice St. Marie; Christinea Johnson; Miguel Pisarro; Marilyn Nolt; Bonnie and Ofer Shimrat; Randa Handler; Peggy Keller; Stephanie Teal, M.D.; Ursi Weiss—and to my dear friends and family who took this ride along with me. Thank you all for your love, patience, and inspiration. (Next time let's get a larger birthing suite.)

Foreword

Two decades ago, noted developmental psychologist Michael Lamb accurately described fathers as the "forgotten contributors to child development." Indeed, for much of the twentieth century, Americans generally assumed that when it came to infants, fathers were largely redundant. The popular view was that the only adult with whom babies and infants have a significant relationship is their mother. The influence of the father was assumed to occur, if at all, only after a child had reached the age of four or five years. Some even began to view fathers as superfluous to the well-being of children.

As a consequence of such thinking, fathers in the United States grew increasingly disconnected from families and children. By the early 1990s, nearly four out of ten children were living apart from their fathers. Moreover, 40 percent of children living apart from their fathers had not seen their fathers in over a year. Fifty percent of those who did not live with their fathers had never stepped foot in their fathers' homes. Fathers, it seemed, were rapidly disappearing from children's lives.

Then something extraordinary happened. Fatherhood began to experience a reawakening. In response to burgeoning research on the importance of father involvement in child development, fathers and fatherhood increasingly became topics of interest to the general public as well as scholars. Far from being seen as superfluous, fathers came to be recognized as unique and irreplaceable contributors to the well-being of children.

At the National Fatherhood Initiative, we like to think we

had a little something to do with this renewed interest in fathers and fatherhood. But so did pioneers like Jack Heinowitz. Indeed, at the time of the founding of the National Fatherhood Initiative in 1994, one of the few books in print for fathers was Jack Heinowitz's *Pregnant Fathers: Entering Parenthood Together*. Since then, hundreds of new books on fathering have appeared, but Jack's *Pregnant Fathers* remains a standout. His newest offering, *Fathering Right from the Start*, is destined to be as significant, both for individual fathers and for the emerging fatherhood field.

What Jack Heinowitz reminds us is that contrary to stereotypes, fathers do care about their children—and not just a little, but a lot. Observational studies confirm that fathers show a keen interest in their babies, beginning at birth. Fathers enjoy looking at their newborns, holding them, playing with them, and touching them. Fathers also say they can readily distinguish their babies from others and tend to perceive their infants as perfect. Overall, new fathers are as preoccupied with and absorbed by their newborns as new mothers are, and frequently describe their experience as extreme elation, often an emotional "high."

Moreover, fathers frequently report being profoundly affected by the birth of their infants. New fathers often describe themselves as being bigger, more mature, and older after seeing their babies for the first time. In addition, many new fathers report a desire to become more responsible—an attitudinal shift that occurs even among men who do not live with their infants, such as incarcerated fathers.

Yet despite the reawakening of interest in fathers and fatherhood, barriers still exist to father involvement, especially with newborns and infants. First, there is a sense among many men (and not a few women) that somehow mothers are more innately suited to care for infants and that a man can do little during pregnancy, the newborn period, or infancy to enhance his child's development, other than to be supportive of the mother. As a result, far too many new fathers refrain from pitching in during pregnancy or even infancy, believing that involved fathering can wait until their children are older and enrolled in Little League, for example, or soccer.

There's nothing wrong, of course, with showing enthusiasm for a child's emerging athletic interests. But involved fathering can't wait until "later." Ample evidence shows that when fathers interact frequently with their newborns and infants, they develop more secure and lasting attachment relationships with them. And when newborns and infants develop strong attachments not only to their mothers but also to their fathers, they function more competently than infants who develop only one secure attachment, or none.

Second, despite the broader culture's renewed interested in fatherhood, there is a continuing reluctance on the part of many business owners to give their male employees the flexibility and time they need to be involved fathers. In a survey of 1,500 CEOs and human resource department personnel, for example, 63 percent said the reasonable amount of time a new father should take off from work is zero. *Zero!* Not even an afternoon off to bring mom and the new baby home! And when it comes to family-friendly workplace practices, too many employers still say, "Fathers need not apply."

But all of this is changing—not as rapidly as many of us would like, but changing nonetheless. In part, this change is being driven by research indicating that while there is overlap in the way mothers and fathers interact with their infants, fathers are not redundant when it comes to child development. For example, whereas mothers more often engage infants in conventional games, such as pat-a-cake, and in play involving toys, fathers tend to engage them in vigorous, physically stimulating games, or in unusual and unpredictable types of play—the play preferred by many infants. Moreover, mothers most often hold their babies for caretaking purposes, whereas fathers are more likely to hold them while playing, or because their babies want to be held.

Research reveals that the "rough and tumble" play of fathers has important advantages for children. According to developmental psychologist and researcher Ross Parke, this type of play helps children develop self-regulation skills, as well as the ability to recognize subtle facial cues—both critical skills for developing and maintaining good social relationships. It turns out that far from being part-time substitute moms, fathers can, and frequently do, make unique contributions to the well-being of their newborns and infants.

But you knew that. You did, after all, buy this book. However, knowing intellectually that father involvement matters is the easy part; the harder part is in the doing. That's what makes these chapters so important. They provide the *information* you need to involve yourself in your child's life right from the start. With the help of this book, I am confident you and your child will get exactly what you both want and deserve—many years of successful and rewarding fathering.

But wait, there's more. As Jack Heinowitz is fond of pointing out, engaged fathering transforms more than just the man and his family. It is also, in Jack's words, "the wellspring from which a more peaceful and loving world can emerge." It is, indeed. So thanks, Jack, for helping men be involved fathers. And thank you, reader, for helping to make this world a more peaceful and loving place by your journey into involved, committed, and nurturing fatherhood.

Wade F. Horn, Ph.D.
President
The National Fatherhood Initiative
Gaithersburg, Maryland

Preface

While strolling together on a crisp autumn day, Jesse, soon to be four years old, wore his favorite sweater and beret, and I was still in my work clothes. In the past, I would have carried him at least part of the way, maybe piggyback or on my shoulders. But this walk was different.

My arm dangled down, and his hand reached up for mine. We found each other and held hands while meandering through the streets of my old neighborhood. I started narrating: "Look, Jess, there's a garden, a bird, a bus, a school."

Recognizing a golden opportunity to introduce him to a piece of my past, I squatted down beside him, eye to eye, and pointed. "Look, Jess. Look at the big house up there."

His eyes followed my finger.

"The green one—there, with the white fence. See it? Let's go look."

I stepped up the pace, curious to see his response.

"Hey, Jesse, you know, that's the house where Daddy used to live."

He looked puzzled. "Daddy's house? Daddy, Mommy, me?" he asked.

I thought to myself, *Why doesn't someone tell us how to explain these things to our children?*

Then I gave it another try. "No, Jesse, before you were born.... Even before you were growing inside Mommy, Daddy lived in this house. A long, long time ago."

A lengthy pause followed. I was certain I had lost him. Not knowing what to expect, I looked at him. To my surprise, he seemed to be pondering the dilemma. Suddenly, he looked straight into my eyes and said, "Daddy, I missed you then."

All I could say was, "I missed you then too, Jesse. I'm so glad we're together now." And I gave him my most loving hug.

Backing away just enough to gaze at his face, I remembered a friend and mentor telling me, long before I'd become a father, that a child is love made visible. A joy I'd experienced once before—while holding my sleeping daughter in my arms—washed over me, reminding me of the miracles of fatherhood.

For just a moment, forget everything you've ever been told about parenting and draw these six words into your heart: A *child is love made visible*. Bring them to mind from time to time. Think of them as a fathering mantra while parenthood unfolds before you, right from the start.

Introduction

As men, we tend to bring more curiosity, perspective, and enthusiasm to the first day of a new job than we do to new fatherhood. Before taking on a job, we scope it out, clarifying the hours required, other demands and expectations, as well as the benefits and opportunities for advancement. We evaluate the setting, and the people we might be working with. Wondering if our opinions and suggestions will be taken seriously, we see how disputes are resolved and grievances addressed. We are wise to do this "homework" before committing to a position that will require so much of our energy.

Isn't it odd that we are not as likely to investigate what fathering is about before taking on these lifelong responsibilities? If we did, we might start with a short checklist that looks something like this:

FIGURE I–1

Fathering Checklist

To me, fathering is . . .

✔ A job with no clear job description
✔ A huge challenge
✔ A role presenting new responsibilities and obligations

- ✔ A time for changing and adjusting
- ✔ Loving and providing for someone else
- ✔ A test of my relationship with my partner
- ✔ A chance to give back what my dad gave to me
- ✔ An opportunity to do better at it than my dad did
- ✔ A chance to really grow up

Fatherhood is so complex and life changing that we greet it with a myriad of reactions. We feel curiosity and trepidation, optimism and concern, anticipation and reluctance, enthusiasm and hesitation, pride and self-doubt, confidence and uncertainty.

Yet the meaning of fatherhood is difficult to grasp. Why? Largely because men's fundamental fathering experiences have gone unexpressed, often for generations. Until quite recently, the transition from son to father—surely one of our most poignant life events—has remained unexamined, misrepresented, and misunderstood by men and women alike.

From the start, we welcome the blossoming pregnant woman. We celebrate her changing circumstances while dismissing those of her counterpart. We recognize new fathers as germane to the pregnancy, yet not in their own right. We feel awkward approaching "pregnant dads," since we know so little about them. We don't think to ask them about their feelings, concerns, or dreams. We simply expect them to set their personal matters aside and attend diligently to their partners. We gladly listen as they tell us about their partners' weight gains and discomfort, but we seldom inquire about their own changes. We fail to recognize that expectant fathers are feeling detached and that, by ignoring them, we push them further out of the picture. No wonder fathers slip so easily into the background of family life, quietly refusing to get involved and deferring more and more to their partners' wishes as time goes on.

As men on the brink of fatherhood, we play with the notion of being a "coach." We gear up for game day, but end up on the sidelines, far from the action. We are not about to risk feeling vulnerable or appearing unprepared. We store our emotions in the locker room. When asked to comment, we offer the perfunctory, "No problem. The wife and baby are doing just great. (No further questions, please.)"

Feeling disconnected and unimportant, even the best intentioned expectant dad opts to take a backseat, unwittingly giving over to his partner many of the responsibilities and joys of involved parenthood. Deep down, too many new fathers fear they are extraneous and dispensable, that new fatherhood will offer them little more than added stress and obligations.

The detachment we men experience during pregnancy is directly related to the images and perceptions we hold of men as fathers, which are still colored by one-dimensional stereotypes: "worker" dads, "workaholic" dads, "distant" dads, "absent" dads, "Disneyland" dads, "weekend" dads, "discipline" dads, and "deadbeat" dads. Television, perhaps our most powerful cultural medium, frequently portrays men as competent workers but uninvolved fathers, or as involved fathers but incompetent men.[1] At best, TV depicts dads as incomplete. These fractured and incomplete figures determine what children, who spend far more time flipping through channels than interacting meaningfully with their fathers, learn to expect of their dads—and for themselves.

Fatherhood is definitely under scrutiny. Broadcast sound bites and instant images bombard us with messages about divorce, child abuse, and neglect. Glossy photos of handsome young men holding babies while clad only in designer jeans are pathetic reminders of how desperately we are searching for honest-to-goodness fathers for our children.

Worse, an epidemic of fatherlessness is sweeping the nation. Supermarket-style magazines cite the latest findings: children who grow up without fathers are at risk for educational, health, and psychological problems.

At the crux of all these problems is a lack of useful information. A *New York Times* article titled "Daddy Dearest: Do You

Really Matter?" states that "although you could fill a boxcar with the research that has been done [in the United States] on the importance of mother-child relationships, you could transport all the work done on the importance of fathers in the trunk of your car."[2] David Blankenhorn, author of *Fatherless in America*, points out that this same society that has neglected to know its fathers regards them as "superfluous" and "expendable." The greatest void we must confront, he explains, is "not the absence of fathers, but the absence of our belief in fathers."[3]

Where are the stories of steady, reliable, everyday men who parent their children actively on a daily basis, who hug and play with them, meet them on their levels, teach and nurture them? We need to know more about men who are happy with themselves and cherish their partnerships; who achieve success but are not seduced by its power; who are competent yet vulnerable, sociable yet introspective, caring and self-aware.

As fathers, we need other men to mentor us in being more effective parents, husbands, friends, and citizens. We also need to discover firsthand, through involvement with our children, that fatherhood is a celebration of our masculinity and potentially the most satisfying and rewarding undertaking of our lives.

Involved fathering urges us to become multidimensional—to reach far beyond any task we have ever faced. It requires more patience, effort, self-discipline, flexibility, balance, and practice than we can imagine. In response to this awesome challenge, we may at first retreat and become Monday morning quarterbacks, letting our partners call and run the plays. (After all, we have been taught that mothers are endowed with finely tuned parenting instincts whereas fathers are awkward and clumsy.) It makes sense to redouble our efforts in the workplace, where we know the turf, relegating father-child time to the back burner. Rather than plunge into hands-on contact with our babies and face uncertainty or "rejection," we may find it "safer" waiting for them to come to us.

Holding back feels natural to those of us who have never

spent time with newborns or known the love of an involved, nurturing father. Unaccustomed to a father's love, we have no direct line into what to do with our children or how to be with them in enjoyable fatherly ways. Nor are we necessarily fluent in the language of caring, affection, or appreciation.

Fortunately, we live in the era of self-help. Never before have so many men acknowledged their desire for family closeness or expressed such profound determination to become "a different kind of father." More men than ever before speak of sorrow and emptiness from never having felt their father's love. Arriving at this awareness is itself a tremendous step toward breaking the cycle of distant fathering. Now we must add new tools, strategies, and perspectives to help us become the fathers we most want to be.

Intuitively, we know that fathering is a matter of the heart, not the mind; that father love comes from the soul, not the intellect; that the call to fatherhood beckons us to give authentically of ourselves, not play out yet another role. We understand that what our children really need—what we ourselves needed—is a father's presence and availability. It simply will not do to offer them some updated version of the strong, silent provider-fathers we ourselves grew up with.

But we have not yet broken free of the programming that has so systematically conditioned us to deny our feelings and our deep need for loving connections. Numb to our vulnerabilities, we sidestep them and act tough. Out of touch with our feelings, we channel our energies into working and accomplishing. Unaware of our emotional needs, we deny the yearning to bond more fully with our partners and children. Operating on "automatic," we have difficulty even recognizing the emotional needs of those we love most.

It is time to uncover our true selves. And as nature would have it, fatherhood lays us bare. It poses countless opportunities to reflect and reconsider, to redirect our energy and alter our programs. Fatherhood broadens our perspectives on where we came from and what we might aspire to. At each new junction, we can choose to regard fathering as either an engaging, lifelong adventure or a melodrama to be watched from the couch. The one choice we don't have is to turn back, for the journey has already begun.

Pregnancy and parenting inevitably alter our lives. Change is always just around the corner. And so, the looming question is not whether to father or not, but rather how much heart do we invest in our children? Will we embrace parenting with curiosity, reverence, and openness, or will we retreat out of fear?

Fathering, with all its perplexities and wonders, is one of my greatest passions. I have walked the landscape three times: first, as a young, newlywed student with my daughter, Becky, now twenty-five years old; then with my stepdaughter, Eden, from the time she was twelve; and now with Jesse, my ten-year-old son, who is pushing me through my fifties. *Fathering Right from the Start* draws from all these chapters of my life, as well as from my experiences as a son, a divorced dad, and a family therapist of more than thirty years.

This book is an invitation to greet fathering, and all it conjures up for you, with open arms. From one chapter to the next, you will find exciting possibilities for breaking the chain of fathering-by-default, venturing beyond prescribed roles, and creating a powerful sense of fatherly masculinity for your child, your partner, your community, and above all, yourself. In stepping from these pages into real life, you may suddenly regard fathering as the most meaningful adventure possible. When fathering flows from the heart, it heals and transforms. Shaking us out of our drab existence, it ushers us into a new dynamic realm. At the same time, soulful fathering permeates our children's psyches, both guiding their actions and endowing them with an abiding sense of security and self-acceptance.

Begin wherever you are. Whether you are a rookie father, a seasoned dad going around again, a divorcé who has lost touch with his children, a stepdad, an adoptive dad, or a straight or gay dad does not matter. Whether you had a close relationship with your dad or none at all makes no difference. You are you—exactly the father your child most wants and needs.

As you read on, you will be guided into and through fatherhood, all the while informed, challenged, and supported in staying the course. You'll find a map of the terrain, a compass for navigation, and a collection of effective fathering tools for dealing with obstacles and forging ahead. Sprinkled throughout are other men's accounts of their fathering experiences—the man-to-man stuff we don't get enough of.

There are no prescriptions here for "doing things right" or "being perfect." Instead, you get to discover styles and rhythms that feel intrinsically right to *you*. For in truth, fathering is not about doing; it's about being who we are with our children and our partners. On this course of self-discovery, the rewards come moment to moment, not at the end of the trip. Now, get ready for the ride of your life.

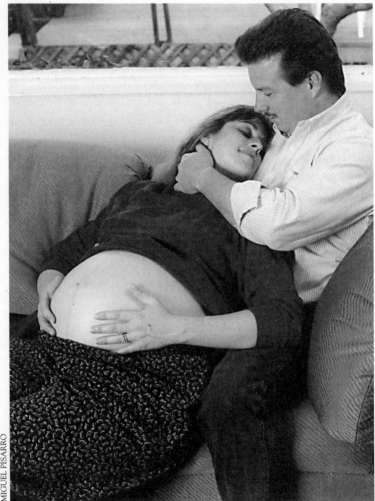

Part I

PREGNANCY

1

The Call
to Fatherhood

*Mothers are closer to children than fathers are. I sure
don't feel as strongly toward my father as I do toward
my mother. I think it's bound up in nature that mothers
and children have very strong feelings for each other—
something qualitatively different from what a man can
have for his child, and vice versa. But I want to be as
close to my child as my partner is. I guess fathering is a
role you don't know how to fill till it actually happens.*

The drums begin to roll and our hearts pound in our
chests. The call has come: We have fathered a child.
We are entering fatherhood.

We start to search for definition. We want to know what it
means to be a dad—what fatherhood will require of us and what it
might bring us in return. Whether this is our first call or our tenth,
we know something is about to change. But how, when, and what?

Looking around us, we see fathers everywhere—on the news,

in the movies, in the checkout line at the corner store. Surely they were there before, but we never paid them much attention. Now our minds have us identifying with them. We watch and we wonder. Deep inside, some troublesome questions may be lurking.

Troublesome Questions

- Why are we men so concerned with working, doing, and "being perfect"? Where do these obsessions come from?

- What keeps us from drawing closer to our newborns, our partners, and our own fathers? What are we afraid of?

- Why do we give over so many of the parenting joys and responsibilities to our partners?

- Why doesn't being a good father seem like enough? What must we do to integrate fathering into our sense of masculinity?

- Why do we minimize our feelings and our needs for more closeness in family life?

- Why are we afraid to be ourselves?

Surfacing enough to dip into a book or two, we are sure to be riddled with more questions. If we really know better than to repeat the mistakes of the past, why are we, as authors Dan Kindlon and Michael Thompson point out, only "slightly more involved in our children's care" than our fathers were in ours?[1] Why don't our children get the kind of emotional connection they most want and need from us? Why do our boys, especially, feel shortchanged in terms of our time and affection—"a loss that remains with them into adulthood"?[2]

How did we men get into such a mess? To find out, let's take a look back through history.

FATHERING THROUGH THE AGES

Sam Keen, in his book *Fire in the Belly*, beams a historical light on many of the predicaments we fathers face. He says:

> We must recognize that men's psyches have been shaped by a different cultural expectation than the one we hold now. Generations of men [before us] were raised on a man-at-arms ethic dictating that males must at all times be prepared to suffer, die, and kill to protect those they love. Within this context, the man had to be distant, away hunting or fighting wars. To be tender, he had to be tough enough to fend off enemies. To be generous, he first had to be selfish enough to amass goods, often by defeating other men. To be gentle, he had to first be strong, even aggressive enough to court, seduce, and "win" a wife.[3]

This backward glance at fathering reveals that our warrior aspect did not evolve out of coldheartedness or cruelty, but out of a historical imperative. As men, Keen notes, we've been called upon to "muscle our way through life."[4]

The warrior-man that resides in us has long formed the fabric of our masculinity. Over time, it gave way to a productivity ethic. In the 1840s, for instance, our forefathers left their families in droves for the factories, where a new assembly-line culture was forming. Consequently, generations of fathers passed on to their sons an industrial-age formula for success. Included were five components:

• Be strong and be tough. (Don't let anything interfere with your work or "get to you.")

- Control your feelings. (Only weaklings and sissies let their emotions "get the best of them.")
- Keep your problems to yourself. (Stop pissing and moaning. Solve your troubles on your own.)
- Stay on top of things. (Controlling oneself and others is the measure of a man.)
- Use your head. (Logical thinking paves the road to victory.)

Our dads took the venerable old torch from their dads—no questions asked—and championed the new ethic, laboring away from home for "the man" and the company store. At the same time, they protected us, planned and saved for us, and postponed joy and relaxation until their retirement years. They fathered with authority and disciplined us sternly, giving few, if any, explanations for their reprimands.

Determined to finish the job at any cost, our dads rarely reflected on the emotional and psychological toll their work ethic extracted. While climbing the company ladder, they slowly but surely estranged themselves from us.

Today, the provider-father, working overtime and sacrificing personal satisfaction and closeness for his family's material well-being, remains our most pervasive fathering model. Many overworked, overextended fathers—whether CEOs or blue-collar workers juggling two or three jobs—are just too tired and distracted to notice that their children are, like themselves, following in the footsteps of the fathers they never got to know. Secretly, they still believe that their most important function is to furnish for the family, rather than connect with them. And in the privacy of their thoughts they wonder whether, despite all they do, it is really enough.

WHY WE HOLD BACK

A good look inside ourselves will reveal emotional artifacts from the history we've been handed. Here lie our fears about fathering, tucked well beyond our awareness until something rattles them. When riled up, they emerge in the guise of blame, guilt, compulsivity, anxiety, and anger. The more unfamiliar our fears are to us, the more formidable they seem. Programmed to restrain them, we end up emotionally distant from those we love.

Instead of adopting the warrior formula for success that we so diligently learned, we need to let nature take its course. And the magic of nature is this: *When fears are acknowledged, they lose their power over us.* In other words, as soon as we recognize guilt, anxiety, or anger bubbling up inside us, we only need to acknowledge it, question its source, then decide what, if anything, to do about it. In allowing for our fears rather than reacting to them, we can free ourselves from emotional paralysis and begin to move forward again.

In terms of fathering, we men have acquired a pool of common fears. To one degree or another, we are all afraid of the following:

- Doing a poor job as a parent
- Being an inadequate partner and family man
- Feeling and acting needy
- Being rejected—feeling unimportant, unappreciated, unloved— or abandoned
- Reliving the pain our parents inflicted when they ignored us, neglected us, dismissed us, left us, or abused us
- Acting like our fathers or mothers at their worst
- Expressing our anger and feeling out of control
- Being less (or more) successful than our fathers

The closer we are to becoming a father, the more frequently our fears surface. Defending against them blocks us from becoming all we can be. On the other hand, recognizing the substantial part they play in our lives, then learning how to tame them (well), gives us options few of our dads even knew they had. Essentially, we get to *choose*. We can stand on the sidelines or play ball, resist the unfamiliar or approach it as a new challenge, retreat from intimacy with our children and partners, or reach out for it.

The call to fatherhood, whether initially alluring or terrifying, is a summons for decision making. We've heard the grievances. We've felt the distancing. We recognize the fears. But do we know the rewards? Here are six of them.

FIGURE 1–2

Six Untold Truths of Fathering

1. Fathering offers us unparalleled opportunities to receive and give unconditional love.

2. Fathering helps us overcome feelings of unworthiness, isolation, emptiness, and loneliness.

3. Fathering endows our lives with new meaning and renewed purpose.

4. Fathering enhances our pride, self-esteem, and sense of accomplishment.

5. Fathering heightens our compassion, our tolerance, and our ability to empathize with and trust others.

6. Fathering revitalizes our self-confidence, our creativity, and our passion for living.

2

Getting a Grip on Pregnancy

It took me a while to realize that I, too, was somehow pregnant. My changes were much more subtle than my partner's, but undeniably real. I think I started becoming a father right after I heard the news. I know I have been on a voyage of my own. I guess I still am. I'm a father now, and somehow I will never be quite the same as before.

When pregnancy is confirmed, we know rationally that we have fathered a child, but it will take time to feel the flame of fatherhood in our souls. Until then, pregnancy can seem unreal. (How could we have transformed from son to father overnight? Besides, the baby is invisible, and our partners seem very much the same as before.)

Fortunately, the journey from conception to birth takes 266 days (give or take a few)—exactly the amount of time we need to begin preparing mentally and emotionally for this incredible new arrival in our lives. And as our babies gestate, we do, too. In the words of a first-timer who spent a good portion of those nine months building a house for his new family:

> Each event—the baby moving, the doctor visits, reading a book, seeing a newborn—is like pounding in a nail while building a house. When we found out she was pregnant, I was very far from being a father. But each experience that followed has been another hit on the nail, another wall framed, then a room...kind of hammering it all home. This helped me settle into being a father.

Thoughts about being a parent may seem fuzzy at first. Even when they begin to clear, they can be confusing. Expect to feel apprehensive, uncertain, and ambivalent. If having a baby was not in your plans, you may also feel disappointed or resentful about this sudden turn of events. Despite our culturally prescribed "shoulds" and "shouldn'ts," it is natural to go through a mix of emotions at the start of pregnancy. For best results, count on being out of sorts at this point.

WHAT PRICE DENIAL?

Sooner or later, keeping secrets from ourselves gets us in trouble. Tom, a man intent on giving all the right impressions, tried hard to ignore his contradictory emotions. But he could not stop wrestling with himself.

> I've been hounding myself that it isn't okay to not feel perfectly wonderful about this pregnancy. I shouldn't be part okay and part not okay. I scare myself with expectations I didn't even realize I had. I've been trying to get rid of my negative thoughts, but it's really hard—like fighting a battle against myself.

As difficult as it may be, try not to push your feelings away or stuff them deep inside. Denying your true experiences will only generate inner conflict. Instead, remind yourself that many other fathers feel the way you do right now. Then air out your feelings by talking with someone you trust, or by writing about them. Spare yourself the unpleasant side effects of suppressing your anxiety—the guilt, isolation, or depression.

Jerry tried to gloss over his discomfort. And for quite some time he thought he'd succeeded.

> The pregnancy was a total surprise, but it wasn't a problem. I just accepted it . . . within about a week. You see, I knew her pregnancy wouldn't upset our plans too much. Not going camping or on long hikes wasn't all that important. Besides, we were *planning* to have children some day.

These were Jerry's words when I met with him and his partner, Kate, ten months after the birth of their daughter. Despite Jerry's claim to have come to fatherhood easily, he was struggling with some very disturbing feelings. According to Kate, they were having "communication problems." She complained that he was gone a lot and that when he was home, he was "aloof" and often "very down."

Looking back over the pregnancy, Jerry admitted he was worried about not being a good father and about losing the closeness and friendship he and Kate had shared. Acknowledging his concerns brought him surprising relief. "I'm so glad to get this off my chest—to be myself again," he said.

Because of ongoing medical complications, Nancy was bedridden at home during the last two trimesters of pregnancy. Jeff, her partner, seemed remarkably unperturbed, even though it had been a very trying nine months. Curiously, when Jeff talked about the pregnancy, he rarely spoke about himself. Nearly all his statements started with "Nancy..." or "We...." I couldn't help but wonder where Jeff was in all this.

The birth went remarkably well. Nancy and their daughter, Carla, settled in easily. Jeff, however, felt anything but settled. His first glimpse of his daughter came as a shock.

> She looked wriggly and rubbery. Nancy just took her to her breast. They seemed so at peace. But I couldn't stop thinking that my daughter didn't really belong to me, wasn't a part of me. Seeing her as a stranger kept me back. I couldn't connect with her.

In actuality, *Jeff* was the stranger. What seemed to be wrong with Carla had little to do with her and a great deal to do with her father's overdeveloped defensiveness—his refusal to "cop" to what he was going through. Having shut down his feelings for so long, he had inadvertently closed the portals to his heart.

Jeff's jarring introduction to fatherhood was a signal from his unconscious, alerting him that something was wrong. Although he experienced it as a crisis, it turned out to be a priceless opportunity to begin evaluating his relationship with his feelings.

It was the emotional aftershocks rattling on well into Jeff's first year of fatherhood that had brought him in for a consultation. After several months of therapy, he uncovered the origins of many of his fears, as well as the negative consequences of blocking out his feelings. Gradually, as he learned to be more receptive to his emotions, he became "unstuck." He has since developed a warm and happy relationship with his daughter.

WHAT ABOUT ME?

Childbearing remains a sublime mystery to us, an awesome primeval process that men can only imagine. We have no direct access to the sensations and biological events that connect babies and mothers during pregnancy. As a result, our children seem to be always coming yet never really here. And the more we want to share in the pregnancy, the more disheartened we may feel. We see no way to "get in there" and become meaningfully involved.

The pushes and pulls of pregnancy drove Mark to exasperation.

> What can I do now that she's pregnant? Not much to do or say, really. I can't carry the baby for her. It's her thing. I guess I can just hang around and wait it out. The good times will come later.

Mark's frustrations are not at all unusual. In fact, he expresses the uniquely male predicament of being part of the child-making process yet excluded from it. His unspoken question is, "What about me?"

This theme has been depicted in creation stories throughout the world, especially those that portray men as procreators. In the Judeo-Christian story, for example, God, a male, gives birth through the power of his word. Later, in Eden, Adam's rib spawns Eve. In the Greek creation myth, Zeus, king of the gods, devours his pregnant wife and gives birth single-handedly to Athena and Dionysus.

A story from ancient Babylonia goes further, recounting the gods' rebellion against Tiamat, the Great Mother. In this myth the gods are about to choose a new leader. Each contender, receiving a sacred garment, is told to destroy it and then re-create it, using willpower alone. When Marduk succeeds and becomes supreme god, he overpowers Tiamat. Swelling with confidence and basking in his glory, Marduk goes on to perform the even more daunting feat of creating heaven and hell from Tiamat's fallen body.

Why did merely one goddess so threaten these gods? What compelled them to destroy her? Why was slaying her insufficient to achieve their goals? The answer is revealing: Marduk, on behalf of all the gods, needed to capture Tiamat's feminine power in order to feel complete and superior.

As above, so below. As the Babylonian gods resorted to murder in a desperate attempt to assert their full power, so do we men pay a dear price when we dissociate from the feminine aspects of our nature and then do battle with these yielding, nurturing, and creative parts of ourselves. As long as we continue to say, "Nurturing is feminine," "Caretaking is her thing," or "I'm not one to show affection," we will continue to feel incomplete, restless, and disconnected from our creative impulses.

This detour into the world of mythology is simply to point out that we can all become wholesome, nurturing procreators without resorting to destruction. And contrary to today's popular mythology, we need not wait until their birth to attach to our babies. There are many ways to begin bonding with your baby in utero, while also drawing closer to your partner. All that is required is a little imagination and a willingness to tap into your inherent feminine powers, as is described in figure 2–1.

Figure 2–1

Bonding with Your Mystery Baby

Your baby, although not in your body, can come alive in your mind and in your heart. Here are some suggestions for linking up.

- Read about your baby's growth in utero, or watch educational videos about prenatal development. Getting to know what is happening in your child's life from week to week will help bring your baby "home" to you.

- Learn about the relationship between nutrition and fetal development. Be proud of the knowledge you acquire. Consult with your partner about the best nutrients for your child.

- Investigate childbirth classes, birthing options, physician or midwife protocols, hospital policies, and infant massage techniques. (For information on infant massage, see pages 132–35.)

- Listen to your child's heartbeat. Feel the kicks; notice the hiccups. Talk and croon to him, and be on the look-out for responses to your loving sounds.

- Prepare the nest. Fix what's broken; buy or create what's needed; build something new, just for your baby.

- Give to yourself. Take time to be with yourself; nourish yourself. Meditating and walking outdoors can help you recover your inner rhythm and tune in to the gestation and birthing in the world of nature.

- Find a time and place to be "alone" with your child, perhaps while cuddling quietly with your partner or after she has fallen asleep. Making contact through her belly, allow yourself to relax, then touch, kiss, or talk to your baby. Direct positive thoughts and loving feelings his way. If you wish, visualize yourself holding, touching, rocking, or talking and singing to him. Then let this image and the sensations connecting you to your child become etched into your consciousness. Relive this experience each day.

- Be on the lookout for fathers with children, particularly infants. Observe and make contact. Be curious and inquire.

PREGNANCY SYMPTOMS

You've probably heard about expectant dads who develop sympathy symptoms. Often, these changes give us pause for thought, as they did for Michael.

> I can't figure out why I've gained all this weight. Although I've been eating more than usual, there's something else. . . . I've never told this to anyone, but when I feel the roundness of my stomach, it's as though I've taken on the pregnancy. It's a funny thing, feeling pregnant together. It seems like we're sharing on a deeper level, and that opens me up to more feelings.

Could these symptoms actually be unconscious expressions of our desire to share in nurturing and birthing our children? Or is it merely coincidental that up to 50 percent of expectant fathers report sympathy symptoms that mimic their partners' nausea, loss of appetite, weight gain, bloating, and fatigue? And how do we explain the abundant anecdotal evidence of men who gain between fifteen and twenty pounds during pregnancy—just enough to grow a full-term baby?

Placing a psychological spin on the meaning of sympathy symptoms may seem quite a stretch. Yet regarding them as expressions of our basic need for connection and completeness certainly beats the heavy-handed tactics of some of our godly predecessors. And although the etiology of sympathy symptoms remains a matter of conjecture, outcomes associated with them are undeniable: Fathers who show symptoms, compared with those who do not, admit to feeling more positive during and after pregnancy, and they end up assuming more child-care responsibilities.

Have you experienced any symptoms lately? If so, think of them as body messages, and just for fun, guess at their meanings. Decoding them can bring hidden feelings to light. Consider the following possibilities.

Figure 2–2

What Are Your Symptoms Telling You?

To get more in touch with your body messages, check off the statements that best apply, filling in the blanks where necessary.

❑ I want to get closer to my partner.

❑ I want to get closer to my child.

❑ I am nervous or upset about _____.

❑ I feel full of (name the emotion)_____.

❑ I hunger for _____.

❑ I am tired of _____.

❑ I feel left out and want more attention.

RITUALIZING YOUR APPROACH TO FATHERHOOD

Ritualizing pregnancy allows you to actively celebrate the new life you are bringing forth. Any ritual will do, as long as you find it meaningful. Until a clear format emerges, rely on one of the old mainstays. For example, visit the doctor or midwife; plan a joint baby shower and invite your close friends; shop for baby furniture, clothing, and soft toys; pick out a special way of bonding in utero and make it your own.

Also, fast-forward your imagination to the birth. Envision yourself catching your newborn, cutting the cord, holding your baby close, singing your favorite song, praying, calling your friends and relatives, then bathing and massaging your infant. This exercise will have you bonding with your newborn right there at the start.

Invent partnership rituals as well. Together with your mate, watch videos about different birthing options; discuss books about childbirth and parenting; share dreams, memories, hopes, and fantasies; observe parents with their children at the park; think of names for your baby; keep pregnancy journals and read them to each other; bathe together by candlelight; give each other ceremonial shoulder and foot rubs; meditate together; take nature walks; dig out the camera and shoot "belly movies"; play music and compose songs, poems, and limericks for your baby. All these activities will bring out the learner, the lover, the child, and the father in you. Release your inhibitions. If it feels good, do it again.

Explore the future together, and the past too. Schedule a sunset chat for contemplating the "big picture" that is emerging. Ask yourselves: What does this baby mean in our lives? Are we continuing an established family pattern? Are we improving an old generational pattern? How will our new family contribute to the future? In addition, reach into your community. Talking with other fathers, holding newborns, and playing with infants and youngsters will further brew the father love already percolating inside you.

Ritualizing your approach to fatherhood will add a powerful new dimension to your relationship and reveal a higher purpose to your union. Whatever rites you arrive at are sure to heighten your involvement in the sacred events unfolding around you.

ACTING ON FATHERLY CONCERNS

Pregnancy is a dress rehearsal for challenging times ahead—years of juggling our efforts to address the concerns of all family members. As such, it doesn't help to have well-meaning advisors tell us that the real measure of our success as an expectant father is the attention we give to our partners. Advice that highlights "doing" rather than "being" and self-denial rather than self-awareness serves only to disempower us, as it did for Ted.

> A man can get lost in the shuffle—not be important, like before. It's really critical for a woman to

help her husband realize he's wanted. I needed more than I got from my wife. If I had been more vocal, she probably would have been more understanding toward me. But I kept it inside. I now see that was a definite mistake.

Even child-care professionals fail to emphasize this crucial point. Continual giving that is not tempered with attention to our own concerns can only cause trouble in relationships. So, speak up. And trust that your love will flow abundantly when you are as attuned to yourself as you are to others.

One area of concern to most expectant fathers is money. Scott, by month seven, was getting jittery.

I've been feeling even more nervous as the birth approaches. I think it has to do with the financial pressures of being a dad. It's one thing to think about going through hard times on my own. But this baby has basically nothing. It's an awesome responsibility to make sure my wife and kid are well taken care of.

Pregnancy thrusts us into the future, challenging us to set goals, reevaluate our strengths, and define our priorities. Concerns about providing financially for our families often intensify as we move into parenthood. The provider-father image casts a large shadow over those of us with fluctuating incomes, shaky job security, or earnings that seem unable to accommodate a larger family. This shadow is particularly unsettling to men whose families are accustomed to a two-career income.

Heightened worries over money are understandable, especially in a nation that deprioritizes child allowances, paid parental leave, affordable guaranteed health insurance, and large-scale housing subsidies for families. But keeping the anxiety bottled up inside can only spell trouble in the long run. Just talking about your misgivings will relieve considerable pressure. A creative backup plan may funnel out even more stress.

Another common area of concern is the pregnancy itself and the eventual birth. Tim, for example, was relieved to feel his baby move.

> I can feel him clearly now and know exactly when he's sleeping, kicking, or turning around in there. His existence is real at last. There's definitely someone there I can identify with—my child.

Paired with Tim's relief and delight was the disquieting realization that gestation is beyond human control.

Feeling out of control is one of our least favorite experiences. The path to parenthood, however, reminds us continually of the benefits that accrue in relinquishing control. If, for example, your partner were to attempt to control her contractions during childbirth, productive labor might slow down; her best bet is to surrender to them. Surrender is an important lesson for you to learn as well, especially if you are concerned that your pregnant partner may not be getting enough rest, exercise, or proper nourishment. No matter how disconcerting these worries may be, find ways to accept them instead of wasting precious energy trying to get rid of them.

As the arrival date draws near, your attention will turn naturally to the long-anticipated birth. With this comes a flood of questions: Will the labor be difficult? How can I be most helpful? Will I be helpful enough? What if I need to take a break? Will the birth practitioner arrive on time? Will our baby be healthy?

Your emotions will run the gamut from excitement and hopeful anticipation to nervousness, uncertainty, and impatience. Airing your wishes, fears, and goals can help lay the groundwork for your growing partnership. Talking with other men, playing with young children, or baby-sitting for a friend's infant can also take on new meaning, inching you into fatherhood, as it did for Jay.

While holding Joey, my friend's infant, I realized that very soon I would be dealing with my own—that I, too, was a father! I can see that caring for our baby will be intense, but right now I feel good just thinking about it.

Whatever your concerns are, act on them. You are sure to be aptly rewarded.

FIGURE 2–3

Let Worries Be Your Guides

To convert gnawing concerns into effective action, try some of the following activities.

- Watch educational videos about fetal development. Read books about sexuality, relationships, parenting, and fathering.

- Watch childbirth movies, especially if you are nervous about witnessing the birth.

- Visit your physician or midwife; bring along all your questions.

- Discuss your feelings, hopes, expectations, and needs with your partner.

- Talk with other fathers about their pregnancy and parenting experiences.

- Spend time with your parents. Ask them about your birth and infancy, and what early parenthood was like for them.

- Create a special labor gift for your partner—something she can keep beside her or on the wall while giving birth.

- Create a welcome-to-the-world gift for your child.

- Begin thinking about who will do which jobs around the house after your baby is born.

- Visualize your new family taking walks, cuddling together, sharing special times.

MOVING TOWARD "US"

Day by day, step up your efforts to connect more fully with your partner. One man who worked hard to keep open all channels of communication with his wife greeted the third trimester of pregnancy with a startling discovery:

> There's more of an "us" now, instead of "I'm here and you're there being pregnant" kind of thing. Now there's something we can both concentrate on, and there's more tuning in to each other, too. Walking around town looking like we're going to have a baby leaves us open to whatever questions, criticism, or advice people feel like putting on us. We're relying more on each other's feedback now. The baby's bringing us closer together.

The sense of a deepened relationship—a more profound "us"—couldn't arise at a better time. The last trimester brings with it an increasing sense of urgency. One productive and satisfying way to handle an oversupply of anticipation is to get busy preparing the nest. Almost anything geared to the homecoming will be useful. Here is a short list of possibilities:

- Get together more with friends and relatives.
- Investigate birthing options.
- Formulate a birthing plan.

- Define your parenting goals.
- Fix up the house.
- Get your finances in order.
- Design a nursery.
- Attend childbirth classes, birthing workshops, and parenting groups.

3

Sex and the Pregnant Couple

*When we found out my partner was pregnant, we didn't
know what we could do sexually or where the limits were.
Not knowing what moves were okay made lovemaking
less satisfying for us both, and less frequent—down to
maybe once every couple of weeks. Right at orgasm she
would let out a scream, or something would seem to go
wrong. She's been changing so quickly that, with just three
weeks to go, we still haven't figured it all out.*

Sexual liberation has hardly made a dent in our understanding of sexuality during pregnancy. Most of us are
unclear even about the basics: Is it really all right to be sexually
active? How active? For how long? What about orgasms? Is it normal to feel sexual at some times and turned off at others?

Misperceptions abound, and perinatal professionals are often
too busy to discuss such personal matters in much depth (especially if we don't approach them directly with our questions). As

a result, it is easy to blindly accept the age-old assumptions about which positions are safe and what should and should not be done. Discussions about sexual feelings, needs, and preferences, which can be difficult at any time, may cease abruptly during pregnancy. Even passion can become taboo.

Although sexual routines change during pregnancy, there is no reason to curtail them altogether. Indeed, lovemaking can offer greater enjoyment and satisfaction in the prenatal months than before. Achieving new heights, however, will take patience, clear communication, and a willingness to experiment with different ways of enhancing each other's pleasure.

SEX THROUGH THE TRIMESTERS
The fires of love burn capriciously over the thirty-eight or so weeks of pregnancy. Typically, each trimester brings changes of its own.

First Trimester
While adjusting to pregnancy, your partner may have morning sickness (not necessarily limited to the morning hours), increased tenderness in her breasts, mood swings, fatigue, and irritability. Self-conscious about her appearance and preoccupied with her body's changes, she may lose touch with her sensuality, and her interest in intercourse may wane. In Jason's experience:

> Since the moment of confirmation, everything
> has changed dramatically. Her whole personality
> is different now, and so is our relationship. It's
> been sudden and drastic. I can see the hormones
> working in her, but I feel like an outsider here.

During the first three months of pregnancy, you may start missing the familiar intimacy of your relationship and feel apprehensive about losing your partner's affection. If your usual lovemaking routines have shifted and your sexual advances are at times brushed off, you may also feel unappreciated or rejected, and begin pulling back. Try not to overreact. Remember, this disruption has been caused by factors beyond the control of either of you, and it is only temporary. Your partner will soon regain her energy, her longing to be close to you, and her desire for lovemaking.

Another phenomenon associated with the first trimester is "spotting," or slight vaginal bleeding, which can arouse concerns about possible miscarriage. Among couples who do have a miscarriage, some feel guilty, believing that intercourse brought it on. Sexual activity, however, does not increase the risk of miscarriage. Your prenatal care provider should be able to reassure you that sex does not terminate a pregnancy.

Second Trimester

Your partner may approach the second trimester with a heightened sexual desire. As the physiological discomforts of the first three months begin to subside, she will start easing into her "new" body and settling into the pregnancy. Now she can regard her new shape and the kicking baby as affirmations of her femininity. Elevated levels of progesterone and estrogen surge through her bloodstream, increasing both her energy and her enthusiasm for intimacy.

Ironically, you may approach the middle months of pregnancy with a diminished desire for sex. Your decreased sex drive may spring from concern about your partner's comfort, or from a preoccupation with the looming responsibilities of fatherhood. Or you may be reluctant to initiate sex for fear of being rebuffed.

On a more subtle level, your diminished sex drive may be related to the changes occurring in your partner's body. You may think, "There isn't enough room inside for the kid and me," or maybe, "There is too much room." The baby's movement during lovemaking can also be disquieting. You may feel intruded upon, as if someone were watching, or that you are intruding upon the baby. The truth is, babies move reflexively in response to sound or motion. They neither meddle in our lovemaking nor feel distressed by it.

An additional factor that can contribute to this second-trimester decreased sex drive is a history of miscarriage, premature labor, placenta previa, or other pregnancy complications. If your partner has been through such difficulties before, she (and you) may worry that penetration will hurt the baby or interfere with the pregnancy. In most cases concerns of this sort, while understandable, are not substantiated. There are exceptions, however. If your partner has had a miscarriage due to an incompetent cervix, intercourse should be discontinued so as not to further weaken the cervix. In the event of placenta previa or other complications, sex without penetration may be the best way to keep lovemaking alive.

Vigorous intercourse during the second trimester can at times cause a small amount of bleeding from the newly softened and engorged blood vessels within the cervix. In most instances, healing is rapid. For preventive purposes, try sexual positions that discourage deep penetration. Spotting after intercourse may also result from cervicitis, or inflammation of the cervix—a condition that can be treated medically. Prenatal care providers generally encourage couples with no history of miscarriage and no signs of spotting to relax and enjoy lovemaking.

In addition, quasi-scientific or religious claims can play a role in the second-trimester downshifting of sexuality. You may have heard, for example, that frequent intercourse and female orgasm deprive the fetus of oxygen, or that intercourse with a pregnant woman is unsanitary and unnatural. Neither assertion is true.

Third Trimester
During the last three months of pregnancy, many women become less sexually active. Some limit their lovemaking because they think they're supposed to, or that their partners are not interested. Some refrain out of fear that the fetus will become infected, or that orgasm will initiate premature labor. Others simply feel

constrained by the physical discomforts and reduced mobility typical of the approach to term. However, none of these factors needs to stand in the way of a pleasure-filled trimester and a grand erotic finale to pregnancy.

Your care provider may advise you and your partner to restrict intercourse between weeks twenty-four and thirty-two to prevent preterm labor. The early halting of intercourse is justified in the event of bleeding or a documented risk of prematurity, or if the membranes have ruptured. In the absence of these conditions, restrictions may be unjustified and impede your bonding with each other.

What are the chances of transmitting infection to the fetus through intercourse? Research indicates that penetration in late pregnancy does not pose a problem before the membranes have ruptured. Healthy couples are no more likely to develop infections during pregnancy than they are at other times.

As for orgasm, there is no need to worry. In uncomplicated pregnancies, orgasm before term does not trigger labor. Orgasm at term, when the cycle of pregnancy is complete, can occasionally kick off labor-activating contractions (that are far more manageable than those set off by castor oil, Pitocin, or other common labor inducers). Some practitioners actually recommend intercourse or nonpenetrating orgasm in late pregnancy.

Lovemaking at term has many proven benefits and goes a long way toward preparing the mother for birth. Sucking on her nipples and stimulating her genitals can activate slow contractions. Prostaglandin, a component of semen, can naturally soften her cervix, paving the way to an easier labor. Elevations in maternal heart rate that sometimes accompany orgasm have no adverse effect on the fetus. Nor has any correlation been found between incidence of orgasm and prematurity.

Similarly, third-trimester aches, pains, and lack of agility need not put a damper on lovemaking. Positional adjustments and inventive approaches are easy to incorporate into any sexual repertoire.

SUSTAINED LOVEMAKING

Partners who pleasure each other sexually throughout pregnancy deepen their bond and move into labor and birth more harmoniously. To sustain lovemaking, find creative ways to accommodate your partner's changing shape and shifting center of balance. The following options are satisfying to many pregnant couples.

Female-above-Male Position

Performed on a firm surface, this is an ideal position for early and mid-pregnancy. Your partner straddles you, either by squatting, placing her weight on her feet, or balancing on her knees—whichever is most comfortable.

Side-by-Side Position

Your partner lies on her side, and you align your body with hers, heart to heart.

Male-Facing-Seated-Female Position

This arrangement is perfect for the later stages of pregnancy, when your partner's abdomen is significantly enlarged. She braces her weight on the front edge of a straight-backed chair and rests her upper spine against the back of the chair. You kneel, perhaps on a pad or pillow, directly in front of her, between her open thighs. This position facilitates kissing, breast stimulation, and lots of face-to-face contact.

Rear-Entry Position

Your partner stands, resting her chest or elbows on a chair or counter; or she may prefer to kneel, resting her chest or elbows on a chair seat, stool, or stack of pillows. You approach her from behind, straddling her buttocks or placing your legs between hers—whichever is more comfortable.

Accommodating the need for variety in your lovemaking may at first seem awkward or anxiety provoking. Try to see each new encounter as a ready-made opportunity to add pleasure, excitement, and a new dimension to your relationship. Take things slowly. If you or your partner is not enjoying a new position or activity, go back to one you are comfortable with; then, if you would like, try something else. Impromptu sensuality is one of life's bountiful feasts.

BECOMING A WISER LOVER

Wise lovers know that lovemaking is not synonymous with sexual intercourse. They express their passion through kissing and fondling (making out), oral-genital sex (fellatio and cunnilingus), mutual masturbation, bathing together, sexually intimate conversation, and sharing erotic memories and sexual fantasies. They indulge their partners with facial massage, perineal massage, foot rubs, and thigh, belly, breast, and buttock massages with vitamin E–rich oils that keep the skin elastic. Wise lovers and their partners take turns massaging each other, as well.

Lovemaking without penetration can be especially meaningful to a woman who has become hypersensitive or averse to intercourse, due perhaps to previous molestation or abuse. It can also be a tender gift to a woman recovering from an invasive obstetric procedure or from childbirth itself.

In addition, wise lovers understand that focusing on the frequency of sex will only create more tension. Rather than get caught up in the mathematics of intercourse, they emphasize closeness, tenderness, reassurance, reliability, and availability. They know that when it comes to communicating love, quantity is far less important than quality. In Frank's experience:

> Wild, passionate sex every week just isn't important right now. Not focusing so much on sex is in some ways a relief. It opens up a new avenue of closeness. Other parts of our relationship are ripening, and we're becoming better friends, both of which feel really good.

As you, too, become a wiser lover and begin to modify your lovemaking, keep communicating. Talk about your changing sex life, all the while letting your partner know that you find her attractive and desirable. Otherwise, she may interpret your silence as a sign that you don't find her appealing or that you are not interested in the pregnancy or in fathering. The repercussions of such misunderstandings can too easily carry over into the months of early parenting.

As a wise lover, you are sure to recognize that, contrary to popular opinion, sexuality need not wane as pregnancy progresses. The truth is, many women feel more sexually vibrant and feminine now than ever before. Similarly, men often find their pregnant wives attractive in new ways. As John discovered:

> Having my pregnant wife around me so much, I was able to appreciate just how beautiful she was. Pregnant women aren't fat; they have a special glow about them.

How can you keep your enthusiasm alive? By checking in with yourself from time to time. Try the following activity, particularly when passionate sex has become an old memory.

FIGURE 3–1

Keeping Love Alive

Any time you feel the need to stoke up flames of intimacy, ask yourself these questions.

- How do I feel making love to my pregnant partner— uneasy, cautious, restrained, excited?

- When I look at her enlarged abdomen and breasts, how do I feel—neutral, turned on, turned off, left out?

- How do I feel about our sexual relationship right now—confused, apprehensive, rejected, resentful, satisfied, exhilarated?

- Are my sentiments less than rousing? If so, why? What can I do to recapture my vibrancy and ardor?

Tune in to your partner's radiance. Shower her with affection. Appreciate the exquisitely primal circumstances of your shared pregnancy. Barring medical complications, there is no reason to stop expressing your love abundantly—in every way possible. Making love is good for all of you!

THE BIGGER PICTURE

Despite all your efforts to draw closer to your partner, the complex changes and mood swings on both your parts may at times get the best of you. In the words of one frustrated father-to-be:

> My wife is sullen and withdrawn. She insists on more and more of my time and attention. I try to keep pace with her demands—spending more time at home, making love with her pretty much on request. She needs to feel I love her and still find her attractive. The truth is, I can't always get it together for her. I need space and time to relax and be alone. Sometimes I feel like running off somewhere. I used to have a certain amount of freedom, then suddenly it was taken away.

Our partners can vacillate from being broody and emotionally unavailable to being relentlessly demanding. We react; sometimes we may want to flee to greener pastures. What's going on here? Let's step back for wide-angle view of the situation.

Early in pregnancy, your partner turns inward, becoming more self-absorbed and less accessible to you. While feeling unprepared and uncertain about parenthood, she is attempting to forge a mothering identity of her own. She is contemplating her childhood, her relationship with her parents and siblings, and her own strengths and weaknesses. (You may be going through a similar process.)

Preoccupied with her rapidly changing physiology, her shifting body image, and her fantasies about the baby, she is also likely to be feeling embarrassed, afraid, hopeful, ambivalent, confused, or excited. But telling you about these emotions in her current state may seem to require a colossal expenditure of energy. Then again, if you've been tight-lipped and absorbed in your own thoughts and feelings, she may think you'd be unreceptive to hearing about her concerns.

As the baby's presence becomes more tangible, your partner may become preoccupied with his well-being. Once reassured that all is going well medically, she can relax and refocus on your relationship.

Late pregnancy adds more weight, fatigue, and physical discomforts, which can easily interfere with your shared routines. Your partner may no longer have the stamina for taking walks or even watching movies, and may be too uncomfortable to make love.

Although zooming in on the bigger picture doesn't guarantee that you won't feel rejected by your partner's current unavailability, it will help. Understand that her decreased attention probably has little to do with you and a great deal to do with her own adjustments and concerns. Catch yourself reacting when you feel slighted or denied, and maintain a clear perspective until things improve.

To guard against feeling hemmed in, take time to yourself and use it productively, for pursuits you enjoy. Taking time to yourself may turn out to be a surefire way to improve your state of mind and regenerate your enthusiasm, as it was for this expectant dad:

> I've have noticed this need to create. I'm growing a garden and I've put a lot of energy into that. The idea of producing something myself seems really important now. It's become a fundamental

force in my life, whereas usually it isn't. I'm also focusing on self-improvement. I'm watching my diet and working out more. I'm trying to be more decisive. I'm reading and thinking more about my new family. All this time to myself is grounding me. Things are getting better.

Personal time is essential for nourishing neglected parts of ourselves and for refreshing our relationships. Whereas running on empty gets us nowhere fast, doing something pleasurable every day refuels us, for it gives us opportunities to release tension, express ourselves, make contact with others, and step outside ourselves to reframe our situation.

It is important, however, to distinguish between taking time to yourself and running away from hurts and frustrations. Fleeing is a saving grace in physically dangerous situations; but in response to uncomfortable feelings or relationship problems, it only complicates matters. During the delicate months of pregnancy, in particular, your emotional departure is certain to feel like abandonment to your partner and children. Any time you want to "check out," practice the following exercise to arrive at a better solution.

FIGURE 3–2

Where Am I Going?

If lately you've been drawing back, staying away, or fantasizing an escape, ask yourself these questions.

- What am I going through (loneliness, anxiety, uncertainty)?

- What is my impulse to leave all about? Am I feeling threatened? If so, by what?

- What might happen if I hold my ground, expressing my concerns and feelings directly?

Although we like to envision pregnancy and childbirth as trouble-free milestones in a relationship, couples often report more stress during these months than ever before, or after. In fact, extramarital affairs, abuse, and neglect can increase significantly during this emotionally vulnerable time. So tune in to your relationship, monitor your uncomfortable feelings, and talk them through frequently. Rather than viewing each conflict or disagreement as a problem, see it as an opportunity to understand each other better and draw closer together in preparation for parenting your newborn.

4

Preparing for
the Birth

*It's been hard getting the feeling that I'm doing the work
when the baby is inside my wife. Childbirth classes
helped. Seeing all the pregnant women, talking to the other
men, and doing the exercises, I somehow broke through
that numbness. Then the more my wife and I talked about
our dreams for the birth, the more real everything became.
Now, with all this closeness, I know in my gut that I'm
doing the work of a partner and a father.*

Just as our unborn babies draw sustenance from the
intrauterine environment to make their way through the
birth canal, so must we gather the resources needed to welcome them.
How do we begin to find these nutrients? By combing our communities for the most educational and supportive options available.

Preparing for the birth is not something we can "figure out"
on our own. We need to engage the services of perinatal educa-
tors and health professionals who can give us solid information
and ease our anxieties. We also need to formulate a birthing plan

with our partners—a prototype that addresses our deepest concerns and desires for bringing our babies into the world. Getting ready for the birth means gathering knowledge, sharing visions, and making informed decisions. Each step of the way we are saying "yes" to active fathering.

CHILDBIRTH CLASSES

Childbirth classes offer valuable opportunities to link up with other couples. Plan to make contact with at least one dad. Hang out for a while, gather information, and compare notes. You'll be glad you did. There's nothing quite as confirming as meeting someone else who is going through the same shake-ups you are and is able to relate to the turbulence you feel.

Although classes are geared primarily to your partner, your participation will mean a great deal. Women whose partners attend classes report less anxiety, fear, pain, and loneliness during labor and birth than those whose partners do not attend. By attending classes, you will not only ease the way for your partner but become better informed and feel more a part of the birthing process.

To locate a good childbirth educator, look in the yellow pages, contact local midwives or physicians, call hospitals or birthing centers, peruse the bulletin boards at natural food stores, and search the Internet. Childbirth Education Association (CEA), Lamaze (ASPO), and Bradley classes are offered in most major cities.

Before choosing a class, talk with various teachers. Discuss each one's philosophy, areas of focus, and class size. Also ask the teacher if she will meet with you outside of class should you have personal questions. Consider arranging individual classes with a teacher you've heard good reports about. Think of her as a personal trainer who will help you customize your birth preparations.

Childbirth classes focus primarily on the physical dynamics of birthing; most do not delve into the psychological or relationship aspects of becoming a parent. If these matters are of special interest to you, consider enrolling in an early parenting class, a couple's communication class, or couple's counseling. As before, gather referrals from people you trust, and interview potential candidates to be sure their approach, expertise, and attitude feel good to you.

Also build a support network so that you and your partner will not have to rely solely on each other. A good way to begin is by approaching relatives, friends (old and new), neighbors, and members of any group you belong to. Single out people who let you talk freely, without judging, advising, or trying to "fix" things. Make a list of your birthing support team and keep their phone numbers handy.

BIRTH CHOICES

If you haven't given serious thought to your birth setting, begin now. Perhaps you are drawn to the privacy and comfort of a midwife-assisted home birth, which aims to minimize, if not eliminate, the use of technology and drugs. Private birth centers offer a relaxed environment, too. Both settings lend themselves to sibling attendance. If this is the direction you are leaning in, make sure hospital transport is available, along with backup physician care, in case medical intervention becomes necessary.

Many hospitals provide birthing rooms or alternative birth centers that allow for the services of a midwife as well as a physician. Some offer doula care (round-the-clock woman-to-woman support) and let fathers assist in the birth, including cesareans. Some offer rooming-in to accommodate fathers and siblings.

Visit a few facilities. Even if you plan to give birth at home or at a birth center, you'll want to select a hospital to go to in the event of a medical emergency. While visiting hospitals, get a sense of each one. Tour the labor and delivery floors, the neonatal unit, and the maternity ward. Check out the policies and protocols. Don't rush. Take as much time as you need to find a place that feels right to you and your partner.

When choosing a birth practitioner, give ample consideration to the type of birth that meshes with your values and offers the most conducive atmosphere possible. Of equal importance is the level of comfort and trust you feel while in the presence of this person.

Midwives, family practitioners, general practitioners, obstetricians, and obstetrician-gynecologists are all equipped to do the job well. A midwife (defined as "with woman") would screen and assess your partner's health from pregnancy through the postpartum period, with a keen eye toward nutrition, lifestyle, family considerations, and extended support services. Midwives trained through hospital or university degree programs are known as certified nurse-midwives (CNMs); those trained through private apprenticeships are called direct-entry midwives. A midwife of either ilk is likely to spend a great deal of time with your partner and your family—far more than the obstetric standard. In the event of high blood pressure, abnormal urinalysis results, or irregular uterine growth, she will refer you to an obstetrician.

A family practitioner or general practitioner also will provide an obstetric referral should complications arise. This type of practitioner would offer you a sense of familiarity and consistency of care, especially if it is someone you, your partner, or family members have seen for health matters. An obstetrician—highly specialized in problematic pregnancies and routinized care—is another prime candidate, particularly if there is a likelihood of complications.

A BIRTHING PLAN FOR TWO

Before deciding who will usher you and your partner across the parenting threshold, examine the factors that are most important to you. For example, what role do you want to take in the birth—fan, coach, or participant? Once you've decided, let your partner know your preferences and talk things over.

Then set out to create a birthing plan together. Make sure it incorporates your shared visions for the birth. Begin by asking yourselves the following questions.

FIGURE 4–1

Questions to Address in Your Birthing Plan

- Do I want to be included in office visits?
- How do we envision our ideal birth environment?

- Where do we want to give birth?

- Which type of practitioner are we most drawn to? Why?

- Will our practitioner recommend a good class, doula or childbirth assistant, pediatrician, and pediatric nurse practitioner for us to meet with before and after the birth?

- Which hospital best suits our needs? Where does our practitioner work? What are the contingency plans if our practitioner cannot attend the birth?

- What do we think about pain control? Who will decide on the need for anesthesia during labor and birth?

- What do we think about electronic fetal monitoring, restricted movement, and food and drink limitations during labor?

- Do we have strong opinions about the use of forceps, gentle birth techniques, induced labor, routine epi-siotomies, father participation in birth, sibling attendance at birth, or rooming in?

- How soon after the birth do we want to hold our infant? For how long? What if a cesarean is needed?

- Do we want our newborn to breastfeed before departing for the newborn nursery? Do I want to take my child to the nursery myself?

- Do we want to be informed in advance of procedures to be performed on our child (injections, vaccines, genetic tests) and to retain our right to informed consent or refusal?

Take your birthing blueprint and a list of your most pressing questions to the professionals you interview. Get a good sense of each one's availability, flexibility, and responsiveness to your needs. Are they receptive to your plan? Are their responses to your questions clear and complete? Do they rush through the interview? Are they distracted, relaxed, attentive, down-to-earth, authoritarian?

Don't be intimidated by any professional. Remember that you have many choices. The person you contract with should be delighted to assist you in bringing your child into the world.

Leave each interview with a list of families the practitioner has cared for, and contact them for additional feedback. Ultimately, the doctor or midwife whose services you engage should have an excellent reputation and a proven ability to support you and your partner through the birth and beyond.

Father's Check-In

Many men enter childbirth classrooms, health practitioners' offices, and birthing rooms reluctantly, not quite sure these forums are for them. After all, until quite recently when fathers began to stake a claim to a portion of the birth turf, childbirth was the exclusive domain of laboring mothers and their doctors. Exclusionary obstetric practices permitted only trained medical personnel to be present at births.

If you are uncomfortable in prenatal or birth settings, examine your intentions for being involved and identify the roots of your discomfort. Ask yourself these questions:

- Am I "into" this? If not, why? What's behind my attitude?
- Am I acting to please my partner? To patch things up?
- Am I doing this because I think I *should?*
- Am I being honest and direct with my partner? If not, why? What am I afraid of?
- Am I participating reluctantly? If so, what's driving my hesitation?

It may be that you feel unwelcome, intimidated, or unsure of yourself. If it seems that your partner does not want your involvement, you could be correct. She may feel vulnerable or embarrassed about being exposed, even to you. Or she may be troubled about being in need or in pain. Just as you are concerned about coming through for her, she may be afraid of letting you down. Or—and here's the clincher—your partner may be pushing you away because she interprets your hesitation as rejection. She might be worried that you will not be there for her when she most needs you. Check for these possibilities, and offer the needed reassurance.

If you are feeling intimidated or unsure of yourself, admit your gut feelings to a trusted friend or to your partner. Remain open to feedback and suggestions. Airing your honest concerns can free you of inhibitions and invite insights for getting "unstuck."

Mother's Check-In

Before encouraging or discouraging your partner's involvement in the coming birth, be clear about your feelings. Ask yourself:

- How am I feeling about my partner's participation—comfortable or uncomfortable? What does this tell me?
- Am I feeling resentful, angry, hurt, or defensive with him? If so, am I letting him know? How?
- Am I shying away from closeness because I'll feel too vulnerable and open?
- Am I pushing him away? Am I trying to seek revenge? If so, why? Is this motive getting me what I really want?
- Have I told him directly how I'm feeling about things lately? If not, what's holding me back?

A negative answer to any of these questions indicates a problem that needs to be set straight. Get whatever help you may need to uncover the difficulty and address it. If the hurt, tension, or misunderstanding persists, seek the advice of a skilled counselor. During this critical time of building a foundation for your new family, refuse the temptation to put such important matters on hold. Dealing with them now will pay dividends later.

Part II

BIRTH

5

Laboring and Birthing Together

I was so eager for him to move down and out—to see my son. Our hopes and fears were right on the surface. Everything was on the line. It was important to do it right, to guide her through this the way she needed me to.

A man's rhythms ebb and flow through labor and childbirth. When labor starts, we excitedly check into the hospital or contact the midwife. Then things turn quiet. Time moves slowly. Our thoughts shift from our partners to our babies and back to our apprehension about being an effective birth partner. Questions fill the silence. Will she get through everything all right? Will there be complications? Will our baby be healthy? Am I prepared? Will I be helpful? Will I know what to do?

YOUR PART IN LABOR

While feeling alone and brimming with nervous anticipation, you would probably welcome a supportive hand on your shoulder, or maybe a task to perform. But your partner is otherwise engaged, as is everyone attending to the birth. So for the time being you'll have to wait and fill the long moments as well as you can.

Now, before the contractions speed up, is an excellent time to take care of some business. Here are five assignments worth tackling:

- Keep the environment clear of unnecessary intrusions and negativity.
- Complete the remaining paperwork.
- Make sure any procedure that is undertaken is necessary, in alignment with your birthing plan, and in sync with your partner's wishes. If she is unable to think analytically right now, present her with options and support her preferences.
- Advocate for your partner whenever the need arises.
- Take walks together between contractions.

As labor intensifies, so can your involvement. With your partner's permission and guidance, try the following:

- Support her in a standing-leaning position during contractions. If she wants to squat, support her under the arms.
- Replenish her food and drink supply, keeping an eye on your own blood sugar levels as well.
- Rub her back, pressing hard with your knuckles to knead away lumbar pain.
- Offer your chest, arms, shoulders, or lap as a resting place.
- Rearrange her pillows comfortably, and prepare soothing compresses.
- Offer nipple stimulation to further accelerate her labor.
- Take breaks when other caregivers are on the scene.

If nothing else, wait with focused attention, breathing slowly and deeply.

The key to involvement is your full attention and loving care.

Remember, no one's help is as meaningful as yours. Remind yourself that you are neither a manager nor a coach, but rather a partner and participant in the birth of your child. Your task is to reassure, to stay alert to your partner's needs, and to trust her process. Asking her for feedback and following her instructions is the best way to communicate your love. Say "no" to intrusive thoughts that arise, particularly anything centered on success or failure. Just *be there*. Take deep breaths, both with your partner and on your own. When tension rises, go into your heart (place your right hand there), feel your love, and send it out to your partner and baby.

The final stages of labor promise incredibly powerful moments of togetherness. Savor them. Celebrate them. Your love is about to be made visible with the birth of your baby.

BEING AT THE BIRTH

Birthing together can be the most intimate act a man and woman share. Paul, a first-time father, felt it as a silent knowing.

> Joyce needed a lot of me—I could tell by the way she looked at me and squeezed my hand. I knew my good thoughts, my caring, were being received and were helping her. I felt so close, like I was experiencing the birth with her. I didn't actually feel the pain, but in my heart I knew how intense it was. We had endured a crisis together, and we had created something amazing.

Because the immediacy of labor upstages the opportunity for such telescopic insights, the moments surrounding birth can leave you dazed, shocked, awed, and amazed. For Ron, a father of twins, it was doubly so.

> A child springs forth, then another one—all in a matter of seconds. This was pure excitement, an awesome experience. How incredible it felt to

have created these beings with my wife. The miracle of it all! Seeing these births right there before my eyes, I felt the power of a spiritual force greater than the two of us. We looked at each other and then at our daughters. Our tears were falling.

Holding his newborns, one in each arm, Ron lowered his face to their cheeks and whispered softly, "Alexandra, Gabriella, I'm your daddy. I love you with all my heart. I'll always be here for you." Then gently placing a hand on each tiny head, he recited an ancient Hebrew blessing for their well-being.

The mystery of childbearing had Carlos spellbound. Swept up by his son's birth, his fatherly instincts took over.

I'll never forget those first moments. What I was feeling can best be called reverence. I immediately removed my shirt and slowly, carefully drew my son to my body. I counted each finger and toe, then closed my eyes, swayed, and rocked him into my life. Never have I felt so quiet and at peace, so humbled yet powerful and full... thanking God.

Bob, while watching his daughter's birth, could hardly contain his excitement.

Ashley's emergence was magical. I couldn't believe she was finally here. Her birth was the most amazing experience I've ever had. I knew she was my child, and yet this realization was overwhelming. I wanted to holler or cry or do something—*anything*.

Having a child fills us with pride. We may also derive a special satisfaction upon seeing our likeness reflected in our newborns. Resemblance confirms our paternity in a tangible way, helping us attach to them, as it did for Stan.

> Seeing my baby smile and having everyone say "congratulations" was extraordinary. I was immediately recognized as a father. Now, whenever I look at my son and notice a similarity between his face and pictures of mine as an infant, I think, "What a remarkable thing to see a part of myself I can't even recall."

Participating in birth is an initiatory passage of its own. You and your partner will enter a new chapter in your lives, placed side by side as never before. In this sense, each child gives birth to a mother and a father.

NOT BEING THERE

Although participating in birth is a powerful initiation, allow for the possibility of not being there. You may feel uneasy and not really understand why; you may be troubled by negative thoughts; or you may have difficulty feeling much of anything. These unwelcome reactions, common among first-time fathers, are usually rooted in unfinished business from the past. Here is one dad's account of this phenomenon:

> I wasn't at Joey's birth, and for days afterward I didn't stick around much. I'm not sure why. I know I secretly worried about me and Joey—or maybe I should say about me *with* Joey. But now he calls me "Dada" and jumps when he sees me come home. I can hardly believe it. The other night I swept him up and hugged him for a long time. He smiled a big smile, and I started to get teary.
> I can't remember my father ever being like this with me. I ended up thinking that maybe

there was something wrong with me or he would have played with me. I guess the reason I cried that night with Joey was that the lid came off my locked-up memories, releasing feelings I didn't know I had.

Childhood hurts go very deep, and most of us keep them locked up so they won't get the better of us. To the degree that we were ignored, neglected, or abused as children, we developed defenses against feeling hurt or out of control. Partaking in the drama of birth can jar those defenses loose, exposing our essential vulnerability and uncertainty. As a result, while intent on protecting ourselves, we cannot help but greet parenthood with an overriding sense of apprehension or fear.

Taking part in the birth of your child can catalyze the healing of old wounds, provided that you are willing to face those early hurts. In either case, be easy on yourself. Avoid self-blame. And take heart—fathering will offer you countless opportunities for personal growth.

Whenever you begin to explore any unpleasant responses you may have to fathering, recognize that feeling stuck, confused, or afraid makes sense in this context. Rather than view your responses as problems, see them as clues that some soul-searching is in order.

While it is true that participating in childbirth opens the door to involved fatherhood, missing this opportunity need not be a major calamity. Fathering goes on forever. And it is never too late to begin. You are not responsible for the childhood pain you may have carried into fatherhood, but you *are* responsible for doing something worthwhile with it. Creating a loving, healthy life for your family is the perfect direction to go in.

WELCOMING YOUR BABY

Imagine being enfolded in the warmth and safety of the womb, soothed by the familiar predictable rhythm of your mother's heartbeat for nine blissful months. Then suddenly you are pushed out into a strange and unpredictable world. The tender hours following birth may be the most impressionable ones in our lives. No wonder a newborn begins the business of bonding immediately upon being touched!

To our good fortune, this bonding energy flows both ways: as our newborns attach to us, we attach to them. Early contact with your baby connects you on many levels. And the more love and attention you focus on her, the more engrossed you become.

Ben was hooked immediately upon touching his son's tiny hand. As he puts it:

> I really loved it when he gave me that stare of his. There we were—my son looking at me and me looking at him, feeling equally fascinated with each other. A relationship was born in that instant. What a kick!

Because early bonding instills a powerful sense of belonging, you'll want to make every effort to maintain physical contact from birth on. If holding is medically restricted, keep up the contact in other ways for as long as possible.

As Sammy, Russ and Mimi's second child, was whisked off to the nursery, Russ felt trapped in the waiting room. When the waiting became intolerable, he set off for the nursery to watch his son through the observation glass. As he put it:

> All I wanted to do was stand still and look at him. It was an overwhelming feeling of fascination, like he was the first baby I'd ever seen. I wasn't about to move from that spot, no matter what, until I was good and ready.

To guard against needless separations as a hospital birther, take full advantage of the facility's rooming-in policy and extended family visiting hours. This is prime time for bonding. Seeing your child grow and change in little ways from hour to hour will deepen the connection that is forming between you.

Home birthers face unique challenges, not the least of which is a torrent of phone calls and visits from excited friends and relatives. To allay these interruptions, consider taping up the doorbell and posting a "Family Bonding" notice on the front door. Leave a pad and pen outside for well-wishers. Record a birthday greeting on the answering machine, and turn off the ringer for a while. Friends, neighbors, and relatives who get the message will respect your desire to nest.

Wherever your child enters the world—whether in a hospital, a birthing center, or your bedroom—reserve plenty of time to create a welcoming space in your life and in your heart. Honor your new family's requirement for quiet, privacy, and at-homeness. When friends and family members ask how they might help, tell them, "Dinner." Good friends will understand your need for sanctuary and will be glad for the chance to feed you.

Relax into home life. Remind yourself that the world will wait as you put everything else on hold. Then let your fatherly instincts flow.

6

Postpartum Adjustments

I thought that once we had the baby, everything would just fall into place. Well, all the groundwork we laid helped me think about what a good father does, but it didn't prepare me for the full impact of being one. Some major adjustments have to be made at this juncture in our lives.

Settling in with a newborn is like relocating to a different galaxy. Everything has changed. As once-familiar routines are replaced by the ongoing responsibilities of parenthood, you will realize that no amount of preparation could have equipped you for this trip, and that parenting is not all instinctual.

If you expect to carry on the same as before, prepare to be unpleasantly surprised. If right now you feel frustrated or disillusioned with parenthood, join the crowd. When it comes to child rearing, there is no substitute for time, trial and error, and lots of hands-on practice. So forge ahead, and steer clear of comparing, blaming, and self-criticizing.

BUT WHERE IS THE LOVE?

As new fathers, nearly all of us must adjust to the decreased availability of our partners. In Scott's words:

> Susan was no longer all mine. It was as if I had gained a son but lost a wife and lover.

Although Scott appreciated Susan's dedication to their baby, he missed having her to himself.

During a hypnosis session, I asked whether he had ever felt anything like this before. To Scott's surprise, he recalled a string of childhood memories, mostly fond scenes with his mother. While reliving them in vivid detail—remembering the warmth of his mother's smile, the friendliness of her laughter, and the gentleness of her touch—he began to see his situation in a new light. Consequently he was able to ask Susan for more time together, and he began to develop a new appreciation for her maternal qualities.

Scott's recollections of his father, as it turned out, were less satisfying. He grimaced, saying:

> My father was tough. He kept himself apart—distant and businesslike. I don't remember ever feeling close to him.

Memories of his dad's aloofness saddened Scott. Reminiscing, he began to sob. But despite the pain he felt on acknowledging his longing for more fatherly love, getting to the truth about his childhood relationship with his dad helped him clear a path for his own fathering.

Scott's newfound joy as a father was evident when, only a month later, he said:

My boy lights up like a Christmas tree when he sees me. This has to be the greatest, most exhilarating feeling a man can have. And it happens almost every night now. Strange, but I can hardly remember not having my son in my life. Things sure are looking up.

NEW MOTHERS AND NEW FATHERS

New parenthood can trigger strikingly different reactions in women and men. Following childbirth, a mother may grieve the ending of her pregnancy. At the same time, she must cope with physical discomforts and trepidation about meeting others' expectations—the baby's, her partner's, her parents'—as well as her own. All these pushes and pulls can leave her feeling bewildered and exhausted, as they did for Mary.

> I'm responsible for this new life. She depends on me. I'm supposed to know what to do, but I don't. I never spent much time with babies. I'm afraid my husband sees my inadequacies and I'm letting him down. He's providing for us; I feel like I'm failing on this end. I think he's angry with me because things aren't going more smoothly around the house. I haven't been making his lunch or taking care of him as I usually do. I'm tense, tired, afraid to show I need him. And everyone has advice for me. They probably think I'm doing a bad job.

Right now, your partner desperately needs your consideration. Give it lavishly, all the while refusing to take her lack of energy or enthusiasm personally. Try to see the world through her eyes. Your sensitivity will ease her transition into motherhood and hasten the return of your loving partnership.

Men tend to enter parenthood somewhat differently. The

birth of a child can inspire an immediate surge in our pride and self-esteem. But as we step into the day-to-day realities of caring for our newborns, a certain tentativeness and apprehension may take over. By the second week of fatherhood, Matt's dad felt the shift, which quickly gave way to confusion and discouragement.

> I was disappointed, hoping Matt would respond to me in some special way. But he was fitful and maybe not too happy about being jerked into the world. Not knowing what to do, I held back, pretty much bummed out.

For Jared's dad, new fatherhood felt illusory.

> Although Jared is an active baby, I can't get a whole lot of feeling from him. My wife, of course, felt a give-and-take almost immediately. For me, there's a nonreality about having a child. I'm kind of detached from the whole thing.

Both men and women have difficulty relating to new babies; men, however, tend to need more of a breaking-in period. Your early attempts at connecting may feel awkward and unrewarding. Still, as you wait for that first finger-grab, laugh, or smile of recognition, know that your child draws comfort and contentment from your touch, and a sense of belonging from your voice and your loving attention. Keep up the holding, talking, stroking, and caressing. The more you rock, sway, walk, talk, sing, dance, and simply "be" with your infant, the more self-assured you'll become. Before long, your child will show sheer delight in being with you.

So, no matter how discouraged you may feel, resist any temptation to pull away out of frustration or hurt. Remember that wondrous times are coming. A month into fatherhood, Sarah's disappointed dad had made an about-face.

It's so beautiful having Sarah here with us. She's opening me up to my love. Just living with her is amazing. I actually enjoy changing her diapers and cleaning up after her now—things I never thought I'd like. I don't feel resentful anymore. Maybe I was a mother in a past life, or a tribal father.

In addition to giving yourself plenty of breaking-in time, make a special effort to be with your partner. Share discoveries, gripes, opinions, ideas, even mistakes. Then get away from it all. Play together, relax, and have fun. Luxuriate in each other's company—no baby talk allowed! At first, you might be able to grab only a few minutes free of interruptions. Gradually, increase these intervals. If good child-care is available, set aside a few hours for a special date.

WHO COMES FIRST?

The onslaught of adjustments demanded of you as a new parent can be staggering. You are earning a livelihood, maintaining a home, trying to amp up your partnership, and tending to (and contending with) a full load of child-care tasks: changing diapers, bathing, soothing, waking at night, and forever watching over your newborn. If you have older children, they too will be looking for attention and understanding, anticipating a quick return to the old routines while trying to come to terms with the new family configuration.

For the time being, you will be suspending your own needs and interests in order to cater to those of your partner, your newborn, and your older children—all on short notice. No wonder the first years of parenthood are considered the most sensitive and stressful period in a couple's relationship!

Adjustments of this magnitude are rife with complaints. The most common gripes of new mothers include these:

- Lack of sleep, time, and energy
- Confinement and social isolation
- Loss of spontaneity
- Loss of income
- Guilt about not being a better mother and partner
- Declines in housekeeping standards
- Disappointment with the father's level of involvement
- Disenchantment with parenthood

One new mom I know summed up her postpartum frustrations in the following excerpt from her therapy journal:

> I wish someone would help with the added work around here. I wish my husband would get up at night once in a while to help with the baby. I wish I weren't so exhausted all the time. I wish I could just ask for the help I need instead of pushing myself so hard to avoid neglecting everyone else's needs. I wish I didn't think I had to be perfect in order to deserve help or a little TLC.

Dads have similar gripes. To some degree, we all feel deprived of attention and sex, excluded from the intimate relationship between our partners and newborns, concerned about the effectiveness of our fathering, and worried about the too-early announcement of another pregnancy.

Alex, for one, was about to burst. Taking a deep breath, he explained:

> Carla seems tired all the time—irritable and demanding. Our rhythms are so different now. She's pooped at six o'clock, and I'm raring to go. Every once in a while, my angry feelings come out. I say something that puts extra demands on her. I know I shouldn't, but I can't seem to help it.

Alex tried to adjust to the changes by diving into a number of home projects, but he remained resentful and critical of Carla, chiding her for being overprotective and reluctant to leave their daughter with a sitter. Despite Carla's protests, Alex was unable to see his part in the problem.

> Carla and I did almost everything together, and now we can't because it's hard for her to get away from the house. So I stay home too, even though I want to go out with her.

With great reluctance, Alex faced the feelings sparked by his daughter's birth. Within the safety of marital counseling, he acknowledged that he felt insecure and deprived, and that he wanted more private time with Carla.

Reprioritizing, a necessity for new parents, is easier said than done. It entails respecting our partners' and babies' needs as well as our own. If, for example, socializing with friends is important to you but not to your partner, consider getting together with them independently for a while. If what you want is more time alone with your partner, let her know—preferably with "I" statements.

FEELING LEFT OUT

While feeling excluded, many new fathers begin to show signs of jealousy. Fleeting bouts of envy are natural, but persistent jealousy can pose a problem. Defeated, a new father who feels left out for too long may retreat, both emotionally and physically.

Jealousy often arises when a mother—sometimes knowingly, sometimes not—keeps her partner at bay. Perhaps she feels insecure and in need of having the baby nearby; or possessive and wanting the child for herself; or deprived, resentful, and bent on punishing her partner. Lying beneath stubbornness, moodiness, sarcasm, criticism, or accommodation may be a reservoir of despair. As one forlorn mom confided:

> I don't understand why my husband seems so dis-
> interested in the baby. He's too busy. Other
> things are more important. Before we were mar-
> ried, he said he really wanted children, but this
> one he doesn't seem to want. Each time he
> ignores the baby, I take it as a rejection of *me*. I
> thought of the baby as a gift to him, an expres-
> sion of my love. He's telling me it's not enough—
> that I'm not good enough.

Mothers who feel neglected or rejected by their partners' lack of responsiveness would do well to speak up. Doing so disrupts the harmful pattern that causes maternal detachment to lead to pater-nal envy.

No matter how left out you may feel, ease your partner's hurt by offering generous doses of verbal support ("I'm here. I'm lis-tening. How can I help?") and validation ("Thanks. You're doing great."). Monitor your relationship for traces of anger, then talk directly about the triggers. Bringing them into the open can defuse these undermining forces.

WHAT'S GENDER GOT TO DO WITH IT?

The postpartum weeks are also the time for coming to terms with fathering a baby girl if we've wanted a boy, and vice versa. Expressing gender preferences may not be socially correct, but alas, we do have them. As one dad put it:

> We both said our baby's sex wouldn't make a dif-
> ference, but after the birth it did. We were both
> disappointed she wasn't a boy.

If your dream of having a son or daughter has not come true this time, you're apt to feel let down. Rather than pretending you're not or going into denial, be assured that your disappoint-ment will evaporate as you bond more deeply with your baby.

My friend Steve is a case in point. Throughout pregnancy, he was so enthusiastic about the possibility of having a son that he could hardly contain himself. He talked constantly about playing sports, being a "special buddy," and doing all the things he had missed out on with his own dad. Then Lyndie was born, and right away Steve shifted into overdrive to hide his disappointment.

Several weeks passed before he was able to acknowledge the loss he felt over not having a son. While sharing his thoughts with me, Steve commented that his initial disappointment had waned, only to be supplanted by concerns about fathering a daughter. In his words:

> I definitely have a special responsibility bringing up a daughter. I'll be really worried when she goes out on her first date—unless boys have changed a lot since I was a teenager. I know about life from a guy's point of view. What do I know about being a girl, or raising one? You can bet I'm going to be mighty protective of Lyndie.

Seeing how bothered Steve was about making mistakes as a father and also how fiercely he wanted to protect his daughter from pain, I pointed out that his paternal instincts were up and running, and would serve both him and Lyndie well. Then I kidded him that it would be quite a while before he would have to worry about Lyndie's boyfriends, and suggested he use the intervening time to learn more about girls by watching them in action, asking friends about raising their daughters, and reading about child development and father-daughter interactions. I also encouraged Steve to ask his wife and his sister what their fathers did (or didn't do) to promote their self-esteem and self-sufficiency, or what they received from their dads that was most important to them and enduring. Finally, I passed on a gem reported by one of our mutual friends, who'd said she attributed everything she did well as a parent to her relationship with her father. Hearing these words, Steve became noticeably more relaxed.

Any time we face untested situations, we invariably feel unsure of ourselves—an emotional fact of life that becomes even more pronounced in the postpartum weeks. However, this momentary insecurity serves a purpose, encouraging us to pause and gather ourselves together. In the process, we can take a deep breath, center ourselves, and design a positive approach to the particular challenge. Refusing to pause, we lunge directionless into the fray and most likely deplete our energy. Worse, when we operate from the conviction that "I don't know quite what to do, but doing something (anything) is better than doing nothing at all," we get caught up in a web of anxiety, never really knowing if we are loved for who we are or for what we do. On the other hand, when we recognize the anxieties of early fatherhood as signals to take stock of ourselves and our surroundings, we step forward not only with more information but also knowing in our bones that we are loved for who we are.

7

Is There Sex after Birth?

*It's hard to find time for just the two of us these days.
Then when we can be alone together, we hardly ever
manage to make it happen. But here's what really gets to
me: The few times we actually do steal away together
are very disappointing. There's not much closeness...all
that "juice" is gone. So now even being with her is getting frustrating.*

Even the most solid foundations can be rattled by the
physiological and psychological changes that rock
couples entering parenthood. Sexual spontaneity vanishes,
breastfeeding arrives on the scene, and eroticism seems as
approachable as the top of Mount Everest in monsoon season.

The trick to moving through this stormy time is to realize
that you and your partner are in the upheaval *together*, and that
the more you work as a team, avoiding the temptation to dodge

issues or to "go it alone," the sooner the turbulence will pass. Now is the time to go to each other—to draw strength from your love for each other and inspiration from your mutual love for the child you created together. Although examining the underpinnings of your sexual relationship may be especially delicate right now, it is a perfect way to begin stepping up your fortification efforts.

SPONTANEITY'S DISAPPEARING ACT

At this point, sexual spontaneity is probably at low tide for both your partner and you, and for good reason. Your partner may be hesitant to resume intercourse in part because her health provider has advised a wait of four to eight weeks after childbirth. Why? Because it takes four to six weeks for the cervix to close up and begin to form a protective barrier against bacteria that may be pushed upward during intercourse. Moreover, if your partner has perineal lacerations, it will take about six weeks for the surrounding tissues to strengthen enough for her to comfortably resume intercourse.

Stepping into motherhood means not only healing from childbirth but also recovering from fatigue and adjusting to round-the-clock infant care. For these reasons, your partner's interest in lovemaking may be low. In addition, her estrogen levels are plummeting; and already "touched out" by the end of the day, the last thing she may want is to be "turned on." After her uterine discharge has cleared, she may feel ready and eager but unsure about the advisability of proceeding. Her practitioner should be able to help resolve the confusion.

Because of the decreased estrogen levels, many women also experience a significant reduction in vaginal lubrication, especially while breastfeeding. Sexual lubricants are often effective and can be used liberally.

However you choose to deal with your partner's changing physiology, don't mistake her efforts at adjusting to it for a lack of interest in you. What is most important for her at this time is to feel at ease with her decision to resume intercourse—free from the pressure of your expectations and her own.

You, on the other hand, may be eager to return to love-making. Prolonging the wait may seem to add insult to injury, yet attention, touch, and pleasuring are not always easy to ask for. When we have difficulty expressing these needs directly, we tend to resort to indirect communication through hinting, pouting, or withdrawing. Or we may, knowingly or not, adopt more passive-aggressive measures such as sarcasm, criticism, or nagging.

If any of these behaviors ring true for you, understand that your partner has probably detected your displeasure. To avoid hurting or angering you, she—perhaps equally reluctant to be direct—may begin to accommodate your wishes before she is ready. But her unstated resentment will eventually surface, setting off a subtle yet vicious conflict that no one can possibly win. At best, it will go round and round, quietly eating away at the relationship. At worst, it will degenerate into a pernicious power play. The solution? State your desires clearly and simply, listen to your partner's reply, then work together to arrive at a mutually satisfying game plan.

It is also possible that in the weeks following your child's birth you may be surprisingly *less* interested in lovemaking. A fretful baby, interrupted sleep, or frequent night-waking can discourage and deplete any parent. Or your lack of enthusiasm may stem from feeling excluded by your partner or your newborn.

It is probably evident by now that illusions you may have had about not letting your baby intrude on your lifestyle were less than realistic. Spontaneity will just have to wait a while. But keep the faith—it will return. In the meantime, plan romantic interludes around your infant's schedule, and take full advantage of nap times.

BREASTFEEDING CHALLENGES

Breastfeeding poses additional challenges to sexual intimacy. A mother who nurses on demand is in a constant state of feeding readiness. The infant cries; her milk lets down. The sensation and appearance of leaking milk may or may not interfere with love-making.

When your baby cries during lovemaking, your partner has a difficult choice to make—whether to attend to her own sexual gratification, to yours, or to your baby's discomfort. You, too, must choose between asserting your desires and deferring to your child or partner. Although this hardly seems a win-win-win situation, it is built into the early parenting experience. Some frustration and conflict are therefore unavoidable. To prevent the buildup of antagonism, think patience and creativity. A good sense of humor about such matters also can be a godsend.

In addition, your partner may be experiencing increased tenderness in her breasts, sore nipples, or decreased vaginal lubrication—all of which can certainly detract from the pleasure of foreplay and intercourse. Anticipating these changes, understanding them for what they are, and dealing with them openly will ease you back into full-spectrum sexuality.

Fathers of breastfed babies often experience some unanticipated shifts of their own. Watching your child nurse, for example, you may entertain a variety of thoughts, feelings, fantasies, and associations. Seeing your partner as a mother rather than a lover can, consciously or unconsciously, influence your desire for her. Observing your child peacefully at your partner's breast may stimulate longings of your own or inspire a new appreciation for her. Intrigued or aroused by your partner's enlarged breasts, you may want to touch, suck, or taste her milk. Although this practice is rarely mentioned by couples' counselors, it can be enjoyable for both of you. If it is, go ahead and incorporate it into your love-play.

Another common concern for fathers of breastfed babies is a fear of being shut out. Jim expresses it this way:

There's no reason for me to even get up at night when my wife is nursing the baby. I feel bad. If I'm not a part of this twosome, then there's something missing. It shouldn't be my wife's responsibility to raise a child; it should be an equal kind of arrangement. But there's nothing I can do. You know, it's strange, but even though my wife and I are home more now, it's as though we've hardly been together at all.

Actually, there are many things you can do, but not while operating from hurt and fear, as Jim is. He feels dismissed and does not know how to segue back into a position of importance. (To learn how to move from fear into power—a skill we all must apply in the interest of sustaining loving, healthy relationships—see chapter 9.) For now, if you are feeling excluded from the mother-child alliance, take positive action. Here are some suggestions.

FIGURE 7–1

Tips for Breastfeeding Dads

To overcome feelings of exclusion or neglect, try one or more of these activities.

- Nestle with your partner and child, resting your hand gently on your baby's back or on your partner's shoulder.

- At nonnursing times, bring your baby to your breast. Cuddling, walking, or relaxing while supporting your infant against your bare chest provides warm, invigorating, skin-to-skin contact—nutrients babies (and dads) need plenty of.

- Take night walks or drives with your baby.

- Be a comfort giver by rocking your baby, burping him, or changing his diaper.

- Shower with your baby tucked in close to your chest. (Don't worry about smothering; by nature's design, babies' nostrils flare out to the sides to accommodate breathing in close quarters.)

- Practice infant massage (see pages 132–35).

A proactive approach—involving yourself rather than waiting—is guaranteed to help you feel better. While taking care of yourself and nurturing your baby, you will also be more inclined to support the nursing relationship.

Your ongoing encouragement of breastfeeding fosters your partner's and your child's well-being in ways you may not realize. Women who, as a result of childhood abuse or sexual molestation, enter motherhood with an aversion to breastfeeding often discover that nursing their babies helps heal the old pain. Nursing can also help desensitize your partner to negative associations she may have with her breasts.

For babies, nothing replaces mother's milk as a source of balanced nutrition, a wellspring of natural immunity, and a major brain stimulator. It is the most complete substance nature has to offer. In supporting this form of nourishment, you both empower your partner and enhance your child's well-being. Of equal importance, you give yourself a gift, for you can rest assured that your child is off to the best start possible.

CLEARING THE HURDLES

Despite the obstacles facing you and your partner during this exhausting period of adjustment, you have what it takes to surmount them. For starters, remember that intercourse is not the be-all and end-all of your happiness together. Communicating your sexual needs and allowing for each other's changing moods and preferences are just as important. Your partner needs to know that she is still attractive and desirable, and you need to know that you are still "her man." Therefore, make contact and intimacy major priorities.

Second, coach yourself on remaining an active parent. If after overcoming initial feelings of helplessness you still feel unimportant to your partner, let her know. She may decide to do some soul-searching of her own by working, for instance, with the following activity.

FIGURE 7–2

Letting In the Odd Man Out

Mom, if you are feeling frustrated or resentful toward your partner, explore these questions and see where they lead.

- Am I having trouble letting my partner get close to me or our child? If so, why?

- Is my partner's closeness uncomfortable or threatening to me? If so, how?

- Am I feeling hurt by him? If so, how?

- Am I treating my partner the way I saw my mother treat my father?

Third, let your affection flow. If it feels obstructed, identify the culprit. More than likely, it is related to the stream of adjustments you have made in order to get on with life. In this case, back up and express your honest feelings about this new world of parenthood, then alter your adjustments. For practice, do the following exercise on your own and with your partner.

Figure 7–3

Adjusting to Parenthood

To reinvigorate your sexual relationship, take time to check into your feelings about early parenthood. Ask yourself these questions.

• Have my feelings toward my partner changed? If so, how? Why?

• Has my partner changed? If so, how? Why?

• Does my partner treat me differently now? If so, how?

• Are our child-rearing values in sync? Are we in agreement about discipline? About how to meet our newborn's needs? About dividing up the child-care tasks?

• Are we able to focus on the real issues or do we get side-tracked?

• Since becoming a parent, have my priorities changed? If so, how?

• How, when, and where do we connect with each other? Are we together often enough? If not, how can we remedy the situation?

Meeting each other's needs for reassurance, closeness, and affection is the surest way to get back into the swing of loving. When you are both ready, go gently and tenderly. Intercourse may now be most comfortable in a side-by-side or a female-superior position that gives your partner more control over the depth of penetration. Slip off to a private place to make love after your baby has nursed. Pleasure each other through mutual massage, bathing, sharing fantasies, and other forms of noncoital sexual activity. Talk with each other about your changing sexual feelings and preferences.

The physical discomforts will definitely pass. The emotional ones, given proper attention, will too. Then once you've opened up to the challenges and joys of parenting together, your love-making is apt to be better than ever.

Part III

MOVING BEYOND

8

Facing Our Fears

It's pretty hard dealing with the idea of really being a father. Scary feelings come up about accepting it, getting involved, learning what to do and how to participate in family life. The commitment part is a heavy thing for me right now.

Ask any new dad about his early fatherhood experiences and chances are he will say something like this: "I'm not sure what I'm feeling. My thoughts are all jumbled up. Different feelings come and go. It's hard to say what's happening inside me." Then he will probably change the subject. Why? Because far and away the most difficult feelings for men to talk about are their concerns and worries—in short, their fears.

The dramatic lifestyle changes that accompany the entry into fatherhood bring up fears of all sorts. Some of us worry about being able to provide for a family ("How in the world will I be able to put my kids through college on my own, like my dad did?"). Others agonize about being a good role model for their children ("How can I teach them when I have problems of my own?"), while still others are afraid of the unknown ("I've been through a lot, but I don't know much about being a dad."). Even veteran fathers worry: They brood about paying more bills, or being too old for the sleepless nights they know lie ahead. Reluctant to speak about the fears that plague us, we suffer in isolation. And in not addressing them directly, we inadvertently pass them on to our children who, after all, internalize much of what they see at home.

But our fears need not lead to loneliness or darken our children's view of life. Approached head-on—as uncustomary as this may sound—they can work wonders, for they help make us whole.

FIGHT THOSE FEARS, MAN!

We come from a long line of proud men for whom combating fear was the hallmark of manliness. Psychologist James Hillman calls this manly legacy our "Hercules complex." He writes:

> We are taught to rise above the failings of body and emotions, To never surrender, to be victorious. We keep our wounds invisible.... We never admit that we are afraid—so afraid that there are times it is unbearable, yet we endure.[1]

While caught up in our Hercules complex, we operate under the delusion that it is our "failing emotions"—our sadness, grief, or anxiety—that cause us pain. What actually keeps us hurting has nothing to do with weak emotions; it is instead a direct result of the lengths we go to in averting our emotions. Pain, in other words, is the inevitable by-product of our compulsive *resistance* to feeling what is really there.

We hurt because we refuse to allow ourselves to experience certain "undesirable" emotions. Then as we stifle our tears and brave our fears alone, we pull away from those close to us. Although our Herculean bravado, muscled and stoic, gives the appearance of strength, it masks the truth. And the truth is that we are hurting. As one father of a two-week-old points out:

> I feel like a babe in the woods—and sometimes it's mighty cold out there. I've gotten so lost in the shuffle that I don't think anyone here really wants me. My wife's totally focused on our kid and otherwise exhausted. The baby does whatever it is babies do, which doesn't seem to have much to do with me.

Worse, we dare not ask for the understanding, support, or tenderness we need. Is it because of ego and pride? Not really. Here, too, the culprit is fear. We assume that our cries will go unheeded and our needs mocked, belittled, or rejected—an assumption that frightens us more than we can fathom.

To keep up the facade of impermeability and self-sufficiency, we isolate ourselves and hide behind our roles of "big man," "success story," "protector," and "breadwinner." We pretend to be the mythological heroes we think we should be. Determined that no one will hurt us, we fool ourselves into believing that by puffing out our chests and pushing ever onward, we will never have to feel our pain.

I recently met with a group of dads attending childbirth classes with their partners. I asked them, rather boldly, "How many of you are satisfied with your present sex life?" Not one hand went up. I then asked, "How many of you can't wait for the pregnancy to be over?" Every hand shot up. Finally, I asked, "And how many of you are having some fears about becoming a father?" No response.

We are adept at sidestepping our fears—often so adept that we refuse to cop to anything that suggests we don't "have it all together." Michael, a "green" father, as he reluctantly put it, came in to talk with me at his wife's request. Holding back tears, he said:

You build up a picture in your mind that things will be positive, and when they're not it's very hard to accept. I've been trying to get rid of the negatives—the worries about being a good father. I'm wondering if I ever really can, and to make matters worse I've put up a shield against my wife because she wouldn't like knowing about the "down" side. I'm kind of lost here.

Ashamed to acknowledge our concerns and worries, we overextend ourselves to prove we're not afraid. But ironically, all this time those who love us see through our camouflage and yearn for us to be real. They feel helpless, wishing they could only reach us.

Our women, who tend to know us better than anyone else, cry out for us to slow down, to talk, to share, to be vulnerable, intimate, and real. The last person they want is Superman. (Even Lois Lane, who had Superman's love, still longed to see the man behind the mask.)

Time and time again I hear women pleading with their partners to go into counseling, "open up," and get involved. Too often, the macho reply is "I don't need that. I can fix the problem myself." Marriage counseling has become a last-ditch effort for many women wishing desperately to connect with their partners before calling it quits. They hope that with the help of a therapist, their men will start to share feelings, desires, and dreams with them. But most often their men stand firm, too proud—and frightened—to admit that the prospect of feeling out of control threatens them in ways they don't even understand. An alarming number of marriages end because men refuse to let down their guard and women get tired of feeling alone and unloved (despite an abundance of fragrant bouquets, elegant dinners, and good sex).

We men are just "getting" what women have known for a long time—that sustaining a close, satisfying relationship requires *inner* work. Historically, introspection and psychological thinking have never been an integral part of the male curriculum. Now, however, we must break ranks and explore the "interior." For deep connections with our partners and children, we must learn to address our anxieties effectively.

In the 1950s and 1960s, television commercials urged young men to be all they could be by joining the U.S. Army. The challenge today is to be all we can be in our *families*. The mandates have reversed: In lieu of following military commands, we must strip off our "uniforms" and reveal every aspect of ourselves—good or bad, weak or strong—stop judging ourselves, and resolve the male pain we inherited. Moving *through* fear rather than trying to defeat it takes more courage than boot camp ever did, and with it comes the greatest sense of joy, power, and security you can possibly know. Being a fatherman is a truly heroic task, requiring you to face your dragons head-on, see them for what they are, discover where they come from, and learn how to live with them, for they will never all be slain.

FEAR IS

Fear is a basic human emotion—something we may have forgotten since ours has been in the closet for such a long time. To reacquaint ourselves with the naturalness of fear, we need only remember our childhood nightmares. Here is one of mine:

> He's hovering just outside my bedroom. I can see his monstrous jaws, his sharp teeth. I lie there motionless, holding my breath. The air is thick with electricity. I quickly shut my eyes and pull the covers over my body. I tuck the sheets in tight—like a mummy. Will my magic blanket protect me this time?
>
> Wolf leans toward me. I'm frozen in dread. I scream out, "Mommy...Daddy!" Their bedsprings

squeak. I hear footsteps in the hall. Magically, Wolf disappears and I am saved.

As best I recall, my mom or dad came whenever I screamed out in my sleep. I knew I was safe as long as they were within earshot. I knew it was okay to be afraid. At least I did *then*.

For many of us, there was no relief, no calming of our fears. Instead, our childhood calls of distress were repeatedly met with indifference, annoyance, anger, or resentment. Such responses to our appeals for comfort and reassurance convinced us that our vulnerability was threatening, that being scared was unsafe. We learned that if we showed our fears, the dreaded thing would happen—we would be rejected (ignored, reprimanded, criticized, punished). To avoid rejection, we became masters at "covering our heads with the bedsheets," feigning invisibility or invincibility.

Now as parents witnessing our own children's vulnerability, we have a major challenge ahead of us. To avoid passing on our unexamined fears to our children and to teach them to deal well with their own, we must come to terms with how, when, and where we learned to be so afraid in the first place.

WHERE DOES FEAR COME FROM?

When we were first learning to cope with life's stresses and anxieties, our parents were our emotional anchors, protective shields, and primary teachers. Their responses to our actions fostered our concepts of "good" and "bad." If passivity and obedience, or friendliness and helpfulness elicited a positive response, we quickly adopted these "winning" behaviors. If being smart, grown up, outgoing, or quiet evoked a smile or a gentle touch, those were the characteristics we cultivated. We took on whatever behaviors were deemed acceptable because when mom and dad were pleased with us, we felt loved and secure.

If our parents were consistently affectionate toward us, we learned that life was predictable and that it was safe to trust others. We also learned to anticipate that our needs would be met and that others would like us. Knowing we deserved our parents' attention and respect enabled us to internalize positive messages such as these:

- "I care about you. I hear you. I understand; come close."
- "I'm proud of you. I'd like to hug you (be near you, be in touch with you)."
- "Don't be afraid to express yourself (be yourself). I'm here listening."
- "I accept your feelings and opinions. What's on your mind? What's upsetting you? What did that feel like? I'm interested in your feelings and needs."

Bolstered by these confirming messages, we felt confident and at ease, unafraid to reveal ourselves and take risks, assured that others, too, would be pleased to know us.

But what if our parents were inconsistent, negligent or intrusive, and controlling? Under these circumstances, the foundation of a child's emotional development is considerably more fragile as a result of constant exposure to disempowering, even if unspoken, messages such as the following:

- "Children are to be seen and not heard." ("Keep your thoughts and opinions to yourself.")
- "We know what is best." ("Don't trust your own judgment or instincts.")
- "Don't cry. Be strong." ("Your vulnerability is unacceptable.")
- "Don't beg for attention. Take care of yourself." ("Your neediness is unacceptable.")
- "Your feelings are at best a nuisance, and at worst a problem." ("If you can't ignore your feelings, at least keep them to yourself.")
- "Don't interrupt." ("Others are more important than you are.")
- "Put our wishes before your own." ("Others' needs are more important than yours.")

- "Don't ask. You'll get what you deserve." ("If you don't get something, you didn't deserve it.")
- "Don't complain. Be grateful." ("Don't feel hurt or angry.")
- "Our love is conditional, based on your behavior." ("People will love you only if you make them feel good.")
- "No one will love you like we do." ("If we don't love you, no one else will.")

Growing up with these harsh, devaluing messages, we discovered that relationships are unpredictable and fraught with anxiety. If we did not watch over ourselves, play by the rules, and fulfill our parents' needs before our own, we feared we might not be loved. Living with the constant threat of being hurt, rejected, or abandoned, and uncertain whether we would ever be accepted for who we were, we learned to hide our true selves away.

In this dissociated state, we developed a repertoire of survival strategies. Unable to count on receiving the emotional nourishment needed to grow our self-esteem, we strove to at least avoid insult, punishment, and rejection. Toward that end, we adopted behaviors that we hoped might contain the tension around us by meeting some of our parents' expectations. In the process, we mastered the arts of bargaining, pleasing, performing, and avoiding conflict. Self-management, rather than self-expression, came to drive our other relationships as well, moving us further and further from our authentic selves until we became strangers to our true thoughts and feelings.

Our fear of being fully ourselves originated in these early childhood experiences. And sadly, we continue to play out many of the fear-driven survival tactics we relied on as youngsters—especially with the people we most care about and whose love we most depend on. We do this automatically, unaware that we are sharing our "conditioned" selves rather than who we really are. To see which fear-evoking parental messages you may have carried into adulthood as acquired beliefs, refer to figure 8–1.

Figure 8–1

Translating Parental Traits and Messages into Acquired Beliefs

Parental Trait	Parental Message	Acquired Belief
Overprotective	"You're fragile, flawed."	"I'm damaged."
(Smothering, doting)	"You're inadequate."	"I can't be healthy or whole."
	"You need someone to take care of you."	"I can't take care of myself."
	"I need you. Don't leave me."	"I must stay no matter what."
	"I am the only one who knows what you really need."	"I don't know what's best for me."
Negligent	"You're not worthy of my attention."	"I'm worthless, bad."
	"You must fend for yourself. No one will protect you."	"I'm all alone."
	"You're a bother."	"I'll never be accepted."
	"You really can't trust anyone."	"I can't get my needs met."
Victimized	"Take care of me."	"I must put others' needs before my own."
	"Deny your needs. Neglect yourself."	"I can't be me."
	"Life is dangerous and fragile."	"I can't trust that others will be there for me."

Parental Trait	Parental Message	Acquired Belief
Critical (Angry, blaming)	"You're the problem (fault, burden)."	"I'm flawed, un-lovable."
	"Be perfect."	"I've got to prove myself."
	"You reflect badly on me."	"Dependency is bad."
Inconsistent	"You can't count on me."	"I can't rely on anyone."
	"You are subject to my every whim."	"I'd better not get too close to anyone."
Intrusive or abusive	"You are not safe."	"I'm helpless, powerless."
	"Nothing is sacred."	"I'm ashamed."
	"Others will take control of you."	"I've lost my self."
Controlling	"You're here to meet my needs."	"I must keep my desires to myself."
	"Your willfulness is bad."	"I must subjugate my needs."
	"Others will not accept you."	"I'm unwanted."
Passive	"Keep everything inside."	"I mustn't venture forward."
	"Relationships are scary."	"I must be very cautious."
	"You can't expect much from others."	"I will be disappointed by people."

The messages we grew up with still echo within us, at times very faintly and at other times resoundingly. Our job now is to recognize that they date back to a former time. Our parents, as our first instructors, could teach us only what they knew. Indeed, many of the axioms they lived by—the "shoulds," "have to's," and "can'ts"—were unexamined hand-me-downs from *their* parents. Although these values, instructions, and injunctions might have worked for your parents in decades past, they may be totally inapplicable to your life today.

The parental messages we internalized as young children helped maintain family harmony, but they were based on the beliefs of a generation that held tightly to the status quo, tried to keep up with the Joneses, and believed that experts should guide their every parenting move. Understandably, in learning to play our parts so well, we have come to regard these beliefs as our own. We also mistake our adopted roles for our true selves, which we long ago sent into hiding. The thought of stepping out of these comfortable roles fills us with anxiety. And yet the scripted lines so deeply etched into our unconscious, and the stage directions so tightly woven into our ways of being in the world, *keep us from growing up.*

Roles we adopted early on to protect ourselves from rejection and abandonment now prevent us from knowing our hearts' desires and from being genuine with our partners and children. In continuing to resort to them, we abandon ourselves even more. The solution? We've locked ourselves up for too long—it's time to break free and become *all of who we are.*

In technospeak, our parents' outdated child-rearing programs have corrupted the files we've kept on ourselves. We are stuck in a psychotechnical time warp, crammed with values and beliefs about ourselves, relationships, and parenting that must be scanned for errors and viruses lest we pass them on to our own children.

Make no mistake about it: Old patterns are hard to break. For one thing, we have grown so accustomed to them that we may not recognize when we are slipping into them. For another, we are reluctant to return to their origins and risk reopening old wounds. Then too, like our parents before us, we have learned to cling to the tried-and-true rather than embrace change, which can lead to growth-promoting opportunities. Afraid to let go of "security" and fearful of getting lost, we resist the pull to venture into the unknown.

So, what are we to do? First, we must gather up the dust-filled lessons we have learned about being a man, a partner, and a father, and examine them with new eyes. Then we need to discard the attitudes and behaviors that interfere with pleasure, intimacy, and growth, moving boldly through them toward new life goals. All along, we'll be getting to know ourselves well, daring to be more authentic, and opening up to our honest beliefs, feelings, and needs. This shift takes great determination and regular practice, for we have much to unlearn.

MAKING THE SHIFT

Both discarding behaviors that keep you stuck and reclaiming your true self can happen in the here-and-now. To begin, look over figure 8–2.

FIGURE 8–2

The Roles We Play

Caretaker	Infant/Child
Protector	Black sheep
Parent	Scapegoat
Confidant	Failure (Screwup)
Savior/White Knight	Rebel
Mediator	Victim
"Big shit"	Martyr

Referring to this list, identify which roles, if any, your mother, father, and siblings took on when you were growing up. Which roles did you play? Do you notice any of these tendencies in your partner? In your children? How about in yourself? Circle those that feel familiar to you as an adult.

Next time you slip into one of these roles, stop and ask yourself if you are making good contact. If you are, you will feel happy, full, and free. To the degree that your behavior is contrived (to gain attention), the contact will be superficial and your pleasure fleeting. Only authenticity leads to deep connections with others. Therefore, any effort that is not fulfilling is best dropped from your repertoire. Try just being yourself. Remain flexible enough to break free of other role behaviors any time you dis-cover that they no longer serve your well-being or desire for closeness.

To move further in your chosen direction, replace the outdated values and beliefs with new ones that feel true to you. For starters, consider these emotional facts of life:

- You are entitled to your feelings. Emotions are not good or bad, right or wrong, real or unreal. Nor are they up for debate. Avoid the temptation to judge your feelings and those of others.
- A clear awareness of your moods leads to better self-understanding and enhanced empathy.
- Expressing your emotions frees you from feeling confused, lost, and isolated.
- Holding your emotions in by avoiding, denying, or repressing them builds up tension and stress. Such defenses easily become routine, keeping you stuck in pretensions and unable to develop meaningful relationships.
- Sharing your emotions with people who are not judgmental, critical, or blaming promotes closeness.
- Conversations with those who judge or discount your feelings can trigger old hurts. Absorbing their negativity, you may become self-critical, desperate, or depressed. Stay away from people who interrogate, invalidate, or judge your feelings.

- Your feelings and moods are transitory. Once aired, heard, and accepted, they quickly fade.
- Feelings are neither black nor white. Ambivalence is natural and normal. Use your ambivalence as a starting point for increased clarity.

Facing the fears stirred up by parenthood and composing new scripts for ourselves is worth all the effort it takes. Fatherhood beckons you to begin, right from the start. In return, you may acquire a new lease on life and help usher in a brave new world for generations of men to come.

ENDING THE EPIDEMIC OF MALE PAIN

My father, in addition to being my first teacher, was my childhood hero. He was husky, strong, and handsome, with a warm and caring nature. I loved being with him. We played ball, made music together, hugged, and kissed. His hug was my shield; his confidence in me, the cornerstone of my self-esteem. I knew how blessed I was to have such a dad, and could hardly entertain the idea that we wouldn't always be together.

I remember the day I left for college. Dad feigned an allergy attack to camouflage his tears. I felt his sadness then, and I have ever since. Whenever we spoke on the phone, his melancholy seemed to squeeze through the lines. With unspoken vows, I promised to soothe his pain upon my return home. But college led to graduate studies a continent away, and early marriage led to fatherhood. My visits with Dad became less frequent. I felt guilty.

One night while packing for a visit with him, I was watching the TV movie *I Never Sang for My Father*. The closing scene portrays a gripping emotional encounter between a father and his adult son that goes something like this:

Father: All right, go ahead, leave town. I can manage. Send me a Christmas card . . . if you remember.

Son: Dad, I've asked you to come with me!

Father: And I've told you I'm not going!

Son: Goddamn it....

Father: I've always known it would come to this when your mother was gone. I was tolerated around this house because I paid the bills.

Son (*shouting*): Shut up! I asked you to come with me. What the hell do you want? If I lived here the rest of my life, it wouldn't be enough for you. I've tried, goddamn it, to be the dutiful son, to maintain the image of the good son....

Father: Is it so terrible to want to see your own son?

Son: It is terrible to want to possess him...entirely and completely!

Father: From tonight on, you can consider me dead. I gave you everything. Since you were a snot-nosed kid, I've worked my fingers to the bone. You've had everything, and I had nothing. I put a roof over your head, clothes on your back....

Son: I know!

Father: You ungrateful bastard!

Son: What do you want for gratitude? Nothing would be enough. You have resented everything you ever gave me. I'm sorry as hell about your miserable childhood. When you told me those stories, I used to go up to my room at night and cry. But there is nothing I can do about your past, and it doesn't excuse everything. . . . I am grateful to you. I also admire you and respect you, and stand in awe of what you have done with your life. But it does not make me love you. And I wanted to love you. You hated your father. I saw what it did to you. I did not want to hate you.

Father: I don't care what you feel about me.

Son: I came so close to loving you tonight. I'd never felt so open to you. You don't know what it cost me to ask you to come with me when I have never been able to sit in a room alone with you. . . . Did you really think your door was always open to me?

Father: It was not my fault if you never came in.

Son: Good, Dad. I'll arrange for someone to come help you out.

Father: I don't want anyone to come. I can take care of myself! I have always had to take care of myself. Who needs you? Out! I have lived each day of my life so that I could look any man in the eye and tell him to go to hell.

The movie had me sobbing. I knew how disconnected and alone my own dad had felt with his father, that he had never dealt with this pain, and that his sadness was locked up inside him. Seeing the film, I hoped, would inspire him to address these issues. During my visit with him, I invited him to watch it with me. He quickly changed the subject, directing my attention elsewhere, and never mentioned the movie again.

My father's undiagnosed condition—the emptiness and pain I inherited from him and suffered with for much of my adult life—is male depression, a condition far more widespread than we imagine. Terrence Real, in his groundbreaking book *I Don't Want to Talk about It,* calls it "covert depression" and "internalized disconnection." He views it as a natural consequence of men's emotional and cultural deprivation.

In addition to the well-documented hereditary factors associated with depression, it is no secret that our male culture has contributed factors of its own by censoring men for being emotional and vulnerable. As a result, a depressed man lives a secret life in *double* jeopardy. Not only do his feelings make him vulnerable; but also, when unmasked, he is seen as a man who has lost control, allowing his feelings to overtake him and usurp his competence. In Real's words:

A man brought down in life is bad enough. But a man brought down by his unmanageable feelings—for many that is unseemly [unmanly]. A depressed man gets hit from both sides. He is depressed about being depressed, ashamed about feeling ashamed. And, because of the stigma attached to depression he is susceptible to allowing his pain to burrow deeper and further from view.[2]

No wonder that men, compared with women, are four times more likely to kill themselves, neglect their own care, and die significantly earlier.

Real's solution to the dilemma is this:

Not until a man has stopped running can he grapple with the pain that has driven his behavior. He must walk through the fire from which he has run. He must allow the pain to surface. Then, he may resolve his hidden depression by learning about self-care and healthy esteem.[3]

Although Real's prescription rings true, it is a difficult pill to swallow on its own. In the context of fatherhood, however, this medicine has an urgency and a sweetness, both of which make it more palatable.

Becoming a father in the twenty-first century, unlike in earlier times, means coming to terms with the realization that behaviors we developed to stave off our childhood fears are outmoded. We used them to survive in families that did not attend to our basic emotional needs. And these responses are neither appropriate nor effective in adulthood. To form and sustain loving relationships, we must learn to operate from our *inner power*, not from our fear.

Fortunately, we are lifetime learners and fatherhood is a venerable teacher—a highly charged personal calling that screams out for our attention. If we ignore our inner experiences as fathers, we will be swept into the whirlpool of changes taking place around us. When we choose instead to heed our fathering cues and to journey forth boldly and consciously, we can become the dads and the men we most want to be.

We begin our conscious journey into fatherhood only when we are willing to be our imperfect selves. This is as it must be, for we are living in a time of rapid change that forces us to experiment, risk, and flounder, all the while facing our fears. It is in confronting and moving through them, not around them, that we find our wholeness, simultaneously developing true character and self-confidence.

9

Mining
Our Power

I was rocking Daniel to sleep one night, thinking about him and me—wondering what he will see in me, learn from me, get from me. Looking down at him, I suddenly started to sob, releasing tears that would not flow before. Unresolved issues from my past and old pent-up feelings I'd never worked out were all bubbling up. I'd been lost to myself for so long I had no idea there was a powerful "me" inside. It was like tapping into the gold of who I really am, which I can now pass along to my son.

Having acknowledged some of our fears, traced them back to their origins, and observed their ripple effect, we have taken a major step toward finding out how we tick. Investing time and energy in self-discovery has traditionally been considered capricious—a task relegated to the domain of women, therapists, philosophers, and artists. But actually, this pursuit is what unlocks the door to personal power, enabling us to become who we most want to be in relationship with our children, our partners, and our communities, as is illustrated in the following diagram.

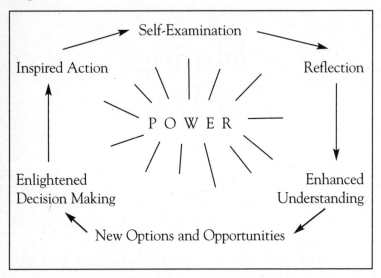

To access your personal power, you must first be willing to take a fresh and honest look at yourself—an exercise in self-examination that is best begun by reflecting on your past. As you step further into fatherhood, you will catch glimpses of childhood memories and feel the residue of strong emotions that have lain dormant in your subconscious. If you reflect on these awarenesses, however unpleasant this may be, you will notice missing pieces of your identity starting to come together. With reflection will come enhanced understanding, leading to an appreciation for where you have been, who you have become, and where you want to go. You will then be free to realize new options and opportunities, make more enlightened decisions, and take inspired action, departing from your previously unfulfilling habits and patterns.

GETTING TO KNOW OURSELVES

Tapping into our power begins the moment we take an interest in getting to know ourselves. For many men, this brings to mind images of a mining expedition intent on finding the "father lode," or of a lube and tune-up on a car. In this context, getting to know ourselves through self-awareness provides the primary lubricant needed to insure operation at peak efficiency. Honesty—refusing to pretend, avoid, hide, or deny what we know and feel—and a willingness to trust our intuition and use our imagination are sure to optimize the fuel delivery system.

Following are a few simple self-awareness exercises. Practiced regularly, they will keep you running on all cylinders.

FIGURE 9–1

Relaxation

Allow at least five minutes a day for this exercise—ten to twenty minutes is ideal. If you like, invite your partner to take turns reading the instructions and performing the steps with you. Learning to relax in tandem is good medicine for couples.

- Sit quietly in a peaceful setting. Close your eyes, and if you wish, rest your hands on your belly.

- When you feel comfortable, take a few deep, cleansing breaths. Then focus on the rhythm of your breathing and the movement of your belly as you gently inhale, expanding your abdomen, and exhale, relaxing it.

- While continuing to breathe deeply, notice the thoughts and images that come into your mind. Don't try to conjure any up; just be aware of those that are there. Allow each thought and picture to move through and leave effortlessly

---

with your breath. All the while, maintain your respiratory rhythm, breathing slowly, deeply, comfortably. Enjoy the restfulness you feel, and know it is emanating from your core—from the very center of who you are.

• When you are ready, slowly open your eyes. Take a minute or two to become reoriented to your surroundings. Then slowly get up and continue on with your day, knowing that you have the capacity to "stop the world" any time you wish.

Monologues and pictures run through our minds constantly, not only while practicing relaxation but also at night, just before we doze off, and during the day, when we're not "on task." If we pay attention to them, these mental pictures, mumblings, and grumblings will tell us what is going on inside.

To access this information, take a moment before sleep to focus on the fleeting scenes playing out in your head. During the day, observe when your body is relaxed and when it is tensed up. Then notice what you are thinking about at these times. While conversing with others, pay attention to your body's messages. Is the area between your head and shoulders screaming, "This is a pain in the neck"? Is your belly growling, "I can't stomach any more of this"? Is your tapping foot thundering, "I want to get out of here"? Or is your heart humming, "This feels good"?

To learn even more about yourself, zero in on your likes and dislikes by working with the practice described in figure 9–2. Discovering qualities that are personally appealing and unappealing reconnects you immediately with your essence.

FIGURE 9–2

Likes and Dislikes

This warm-up exercise jump-starts your self-awareness by helping you focus on your natural responses to your surroundings.

Practice it regularly at home, on the job, or anywhere else you happen to be.

- Sit in a quiet, comfortable spot and focus on your breath. Relax, this time with your eyes open.

- Slowly look around you. As something in your environment catches your attention, let yourself respond to it. Do you like this object or not? Is it interesting, pleasing, irritating? What do you notice about its color, shape, scent, pitch, texture?

- Now scan your surroundings again until something else draws your attention. Observe how *this* object affects you, and state your reaction in words, such as "I like this painting because it's large (vibrant, modern, classical)" or "It's too bright (abstract, bold, subtle)." Don't be wishy-washy; let yourself react.

After practicing this exercise diligently for two weeks, Nicholas, mired in food shopping, evening "diaper duty," and an arduous work schedule, could feel the results. That Saturday morning, armed with paper and pencil, he began planning an addition to his house. In his words:

> I kept thinking about designing a deck. I could almost feel the smoothness of the long planks of wood and hear the steady rhythm of the hammer. I've discovered how important it is for me to know what feels good and to just do it—taking my own leads, being creative again.

Once you have begun acting on your awareness of objects you like and dislike, look inward once more, this time reflecting on your responses to events and interactions. For assistance, periodically review your day following the instructions given in figure 9–3.

Figure 9–3

The Day's Inventory

Conducting an inventory at the end of the day will help you identify how your experiences affect you. To gain the most from this exercise, be brutally honest.

• Thinking back on your day, pick one experience you enjoyed (showering, eating lunch, starting or finishing a task, spending time with someone special) and one experience you would just as soon never repeat (waiting in line, being cut off in traffic, bickering with a coworker). In each instance, identify why you felt the way you did.

• Reviewing the many events of your day, answer these questions:

What bored you? What stimulated you? What pleased you? What bothered, annoyed, frustrated, or upset you? Why?

Which events were meaningful to you? Which were not? What accounts for the differences?

Who do you look forward to seeing again? Who would you rather not see? Why?

Do you have lingering thoughts, frustrations, or other unresolved feelings from your day? Are there things you wish you had said or done but didn't? What? To whom? Do you want to get back to them tomorrow? If not, why?

What do you want to do differently tomorrow?

Based on what you learned from these two self-awareness exercises, state your conclusions to your partner or record them in a fathering journal. As you do, refuse to analyze or discredit your statements, for they are your truths. It is your right to dislike aspects of your world, including the attitudes and behaviors of others. In fact, your integrity demands that you do since your thoughts, interests, and wishes for the future are part of *who you are*. Not only do they belong to you, they insist on coming to expression. Do not minimize them—and by all means, don't give them away.

LETTING OURSELVES BE KNOWN

Finding the gold at the center of our being is only half of the adventure; extracting and disseminating it is what brightens our lives and those of our loved ones. Why? Because in manifesting our power we can find our unique direction and fulfillment. And when we are in our power, our partners and children can appreciate us for who we truly are—which, as nature would have it, is among their greatest desires.

The remaining exercises in this chapter are therefore designed to support you in revealing yourself to your partner. The more you lay bare your inner universe, the better she will be at understanding you, the more relieved she will be to stop expending so much energy in guesswork, and the sooner your bond with her will strengthen.

FIGURE 9–4

Sharing Powerfully with Your Partner

For increased harmony and happiness at home, devote a few minutes each day to this exercise.

- Reflect on your relationship with your partner. What do you like and appreciate about her? What bothers you the most about her? Why?

- How does it feel to greet her? To say goodbye? To be alone with her? To be together with mutual friends?

- Think of specific moments you've spent together recently. Did you feel "at one," in sync, or estranged? Were you heard and appreciated, or taken for granted and dismissed? How did you react? Was it in keeping with your true feelings? If not, why?

- Convey this information to your partner.

If you, like most of us, are a novice at identifying feelings toward a loved one and giving voice to them, work with these two warm-up practices. To pinpoint some of your present feelings toward your partner, complete these sentences:

- When she says (does) _____, I feel
  _____.

- What I do (say) in response to her is
  _____.

- What I want to do (say) is
  _____.

To overcome difficulty in expressing yourself to your partner, try this:

- Visualize your partner sitting nearby and listening attentively to you as you speak comfortably about something that is on your mind.
- See and hear yourself asking her for what you want. Then visualize her positive response.
- Enjoy the results.

Visualizations—jaunts into our imagination—provide a perfect medium for bringing desires to fruition. Even athletes rely on them, relaxing and imagining their desired performance outcome, almost always with great success. With a little practice in identifying your feelings and visualizing the positive results, you will soon feel at ease speaking from your power.

To come from a place of power, we must also stop censoring ourselves. Although biting our tongues may seem inconsequential in the moment, if we suppress feelings and needs for too long they turn sour. The piles of unfinished business we amass eventually clutter up our relationships and interfere with the movement of our lives. Using the exercise below, strive to clear out the messes sooner rather than later.

FIGURE 9–5

Calling It Quits on Self-Policing

To liberate old parts of yourself still locked up inside, follow these steps.

- Think about the opinions, sentiments, concerns, or requests you avoid talking about with your partner, including the "little things" that may not seem worth mentioning. Then identify the three subjects you are most reluctant to talk about.

- What do you suppose might happen if you brought these subjects up right now? What happened in other relationships when you expressed your real feelings, concerns, or opinions about such matters? (Since you are still reluctant to air these sentiments, you can bet they were poorly received before.)

- Ask yourself: "Is the situation with my partner the same as these earlier ones? If my father (mother, previous girlfriend) didn't seem to care about my feelings, does this mean my partner won't?" (Chances are that the answer is "no" and her response will be far more satisfying than you might imagine. After all, she is your love—not someone from the past.)

- Do some soul searching by asking: "When I censor myself with my partner, do I become tentative, distant, or resentful of her?" (Most likely, you do.) "Do I express my reactions directly or indirectly?" (You can bet the answer is "indirectly.") "When I am indirect, how does my behavior affect our relationship?" (Things will improve by letting down your guard and taking a risk.)

- As soon as you feel at ease talking about the "unspeakable," fire your inner police.

Even with a growing ability to speak from your heart and an easing of self-censoring, you may be tempted to avoid stating your desires directly. After all, we men have been encouraged to satisfy our partners' desires before our own. But what we were not told is that loving women deeply desire to know their men and give them what they most want.

Stating your desires clearly and directly may not come easily at first. But as surely as a strenuous spring training often leads to a successful baseball season, your initial attempts to state your peace are likely to give way to loud and clear pronouncements that are surprisingly well received. To gear up, practice the following exercise once a week.

Figure 9–6

Announcing Your Wants

To talk about your desires face-to-face with your partner, use this two-step technique.

- List the things you most want in life. Begin with those you are certain about (a car with good gas mileage, a nice home, a vacation). Then move on to your relationship wants (to be heard, hugged, passionate together). Be concrete and firm. For instance, write, "I want you to listen to me" or "I want a hug" or "I want to make love," rather than "I think I'd like some attention."

- Share your list with your partner. Clear personal statements such as "I want to go out with you tonight" or "I really want to talk with you" can go a long way toward helping you be real.

Although getting to know ourselves and letting ourselves be known to others can entail seemingly great risk, the rewards are boundless. In exploring the nooks and crannies of our inner worlds, we encounter treasures, unlock mysteries, revisit precious moments of faith and innocence, unearth secrets, and set our dreams free to soar. Best of all, we discover the uniqueness of who we really are.

Always this prospecting enhances our feelings of well-being. For example, while digging, you may recall a time when you burst through your front door exuding pure, unchecked enthusiasm, curiosity, or amazement. Reclaiming these feelings now can infuse your present-day relationships with joy. Also, your child will take you back there a thousand times if you let her. Regardless of where these connecting behaviors originate—whether with you, your partner, or your child—they will quickly stir up excitement, and passing it on is powerful fathering.

10

What Our Partners Really Want

She thinks I'm attacking her, but I'm not. I'm just trying to let her know how I feel. When she insists that I'm angry and critical of her, what can I say? I'm so frustrated. I can't get through to her. I don't know if it's her or me. . . . We need some new way of talking, 'cause I'm doing everything I can think of and it's just not working.

Let's face it, we want to please our partners but, much to our surprise, many of the behaviors we think will be pleasing are not well received. One reason for this discrepancy is that, as we now know, we've been wired to keep our desires to ourselves and play out hollow roles. Another reason is that few of us have ever been shown how to listen effectively, communicate meaningfully, or "team up" away from the playing field. What do we do, for example, when we see our partners upset? Do we respond with caring gestures and gentle questions, or by probing, challenging, or worse, tuning it out?

Although there are no positive or negative emotions, there are definitely effective and ineffective ways to communicate with our loved ones. To avoid "disconnects" and maximize family harmony, we need to brush up on our messaging skills and team-building efforts. With improved proficiency in these areas, we will be better equipped to give our partners what they want rather than what we mistakenly think they want.

LISTENING PITFALLS
Good listening is rare in today's harried world because the roads leading to reliable contact are riddled with snares and detours. Here are six listening pitfalls that even the most well meaning of us fall into from time to time.

The Eager Beaver (Half-Heartedness)
The eager beaver wants very much to help but is preoccupied. Trying to be attentive when we are distracted almost always spells trouble. We can only be available to our partners when we are fully present and accounted for, both mentally and emotionally. Any time you are unable to move full-throttle into active listening, it's better to wait. Tell your partner that you hear what she is saying but are unable to give it adequate attention right now. Briefly explain why and agree on a better time. Then slow down and take a few minutes to yourself so that you can be more receptive later.

The White Knight (Advising, Solving, Doing)
Although we were raised to be white knights capable of rescuing damsels in distress, we certainly are not responsible for counseling our partners, solving their problems, or even making them feel better. In fact, these tactics only divert our partners from mastering their dilemmas themselves. And the more we try to solve problems or salve feelings, the more resistance we encounter. While listening to your partner, give support, not

solutions. Provide an arena safe enough for her to open up and validating enough for her to reach her own conclusions, which is what she wants to do anyway.

The Moralist (Dispensing "Shoulds," "Musts," Warnings)

Preaching usually causes others to pull back. Moral pronouncements—"shoulds" and "shouldn'ts," "musts" and "mustn'ts"—are certain to alienate your partner, who has probably had her fill of mandates and dire predictions from parents, teachers, relatives, and society. What she would like from you is a vote of confidence, not directives.

The Shrink (Explaining, Interrogating, Interpreting, Asking Why)

No one likes to be analyzed by a loved one. Tell your partner what she is feeling, or interpret her motives and actions, and you are sure to be stonewalled. Approach her with a barrage of *whys*—"Why don't you . . . ?" or "Why do you . . . ?"—and she may shut down right before your eyes. Instead, replace the whys with whats or hows, as in "What are you thinking?" or "How are you feeling?" Be curious rather than intrusive, and she will be much more receptive.

The Critical Parent (Judging, Blaming, Lecturing, Name Calling)

Guard against any tendency to condemn, accuse, instruct, or scold, no matter how constructive your pronouncements may at first appear. Critiques —"How could you feel (do) that?" or "You always (never) . . ." or "That's good (bad), smart (stupid), right (wrong) . . ." or "You're lazy (selfish, immature, a nag) . . . "—are land mines that will eventually blow up in your face. They imply, "I'm okay; you're not." Such psychological jabs may hurl your partner back to the corner she retreated into each time her childhood self-expression was criticized or punished. To maintain good contact, step back and ask yourself, "Why am I feeling critical right now?" (Behind most criticism is hurt or fear.) Or ask, "Where did I learn to criticize?" and "Is this how I want to treat my partner or is it an artifact from my childhood?" If it proves to be an ancient relic, discard it and move on to more rewarding forms of communication.

The Invalidator (Discounting, Denying, Belittling)

Declare a moratorium on put-downs and other dismissing remarks, such as "You don't really mean (feel, think) that, do you?" or "Forget about it. Let it go—it's not that important. You're just upset (tired, PMS-ing). You'll feel better tomorrow." These types of responses end up negating your partner's experience and will feel rejecting to her; "you" statements generally point the finger, causing others to feel ashamed. If instead you acknowledge your partner's experience and offer feedback framed in "I" statements, she will feel more accepted and loved.

MEANINGFUL COMMUNICATION

Steering clear of listening pitfalls eases the way to a helpful exchange of information and a sharing of real feelings, both of which improve our contact with our partners. In addition, they set the stage for communicating more effectively with our children and others. Following are several tips for keeping the channels of communication open and inviting.

Use "Connectors"

Whenever possible, respond with connectors—short, simple phrases that convey your interest and promote meaningful dialogue. Here are some examples:

- "What's happening, hon? You look beat. Do you want to talk?"
- "Uh-huh, I see. I'm with you."
- "Really? Tell me more about it."
- "How was that for you?"
- "What was it like?"
- "Hmm, interesting."
- "I'm sorry you're upset."
- "Is there something I can do?"

Facilitate Your Understanding

Any time you are unclear about your partner's message, lift the fog by asking caring questions. Good facilitators include such phrases as "It sounds like _____," "Are you saying that _____?" "Is it that _____?" and "I'm wondering (thinking, sensing, feeling) _____" For practice, try the exercise described in figure 10–1.

FIGURE 10–1

Facilitating

This communication technique sharpens clarity and boosts comprehension.

- Assume the role of message sender. Your partner is the receiver, or listener. As sender, choose a problem to talk about. For a few minutes, share your thoughts and feelings on the matter while your partner responds only with facilitators.

- Now switch roles and repeat the previous step.

- Tell your partner one thing she did as a listener that you appreciated. Then ask her to do the same for you.

Mirror Feelings

Mirroring feelings entails listening "between the words" to extract the unstated emotion, then restating the message to reflect that emotion. Searching for hidden feelings can be challenging. For example, your partner may say, "Gosh, I've gained only ten pounds, and I haven't felt the baby move yet. Jane's gained at least fifteen pounds, and her baby's kicking all the time." Your partner's underlying point might be, "I'm worried (concerned, insecure)" or "I'm feeling alone and different" or "I need your reassurance that everything's okay."

Or your partner may say, "It seems our two-year-old is always crying. I just don't know what to do about it." In this instance, the emotional undertow might be, "I'm really frustrated (worried, irritated)" or "I'm afraid I'm not an effective parent" or "I'm feeling upset, scared, and unsure of myself" or "I'd really like your help with this."

To identify your partner's unspoken feeling, begin by asking caring questions, using facilitators such as "Honey, are you saying that _____?" or "It sounds like you may be feeling _____ about _____." After ruling out one or two possibilities, proceed to mirror another feeling by restating her message in your own words, all the while reflecting back the emotion. For example, when your baby's been crying a great deal, you might say, "It's really hard to know how to handle so much crying, isn't it?" If your comment rings true, your partner will feel heard and understood—a sure incentive for her to share more. At this point she may explain, "Yes, it's like _____." On the other hand, if your statement misses the mark, no harm has been done. Your partner may reply, "No, that's not it. It's more like _____." In either event, be sure to confirm her updated message, saying, "Oh, it's like _____ for you, huh?"

Mirroring your partner's feelings will let her know that you are trying to put yourself in her place and are taking her feelings seriously. She is certain to regard your efforts as a much appreciated labor of love. If mirroring seems difficult at first, work with this exercise.

FIGURE 10–2

Mirroring

This communication technique relies on reflecting an unexpressed feeling to unearth the deeper meaning of a message.

- Assuming the role of sender, relay a personal message, leaving your underlying feeling unexpressed.

- Your partner, as listener, restates the message, attempting to mirror the unstated feeling.

- Now switch roles and repeat the previous steps.

One pregnant couple I know combined facilitating and mirroring in the following dialogue.

Sender: I spoke to my mother again, and she just went on and on about her gardening and about Dad's heart condition.

Listener (*trying a facilitator*): It sounds like she's concerned about your father's health. Are you?

Sender: Yes, but that's not it. It's that my mother and I were talking, and she kept carrying on about her gardening and Dad's health.

Listener (*trying another facilitator*): Is your mother upsetting you?

Sender: Yeah. You know, whenever I call her these days, she just goes on and on about their stuff.

Listener (*restating the message in his own words*): She just goes on and on about herself and your dad when you call her?

Sender: Yes, she's totally wrapped up in the two of them. She hasn't visited me or even asked about the pregnancy, and that really hurts. [*Deeper message revealed*]

Listener: I hear you, honey. I'm sorry you're hurting about that.

A FOUNDATION FOR TEAMWORK

Too often, we jump into growing a family without taking time to prepare a solid foundation for it to rest on. We become so engrossed in imagining and designing our dream home that we skip over the nitty-gritty details of making it secure. For our families to thrive, we must plan *together* and work as *partners* right from the start—something nearly every new mother longs for. Successful teamwork evolves naturally as a result of drawing up agreements together, scheduling one-on-one time together, and a handful of other efforts geared toward cementing a solid base for a mutually rewarding partnering and parenting experience.

Composing a Partnering Agreement

To foster singleness of vision with your partner as you move into all-out parenting, agree on some relationship ground rules. Write them down, and refer to them whenever either one of you is blown off course. Be sure to revise your agreement as needed.

For best results, your initial partnering agreement should be short and easy to remember. Following is a sample document.

FIGURE 10–3

Our Partnering Agreement

We will support and encourage each other to

- Be honest and authentic rather than passive and accommodating

- Be "up front" with our expectations and feelings

- Ask for what we want and need

- Check out all assumptions

- Keep our promises

- Be fallible—make mistakes, be unreasonable, admit what we don't know, be unavailable and moody at times

- Say "no" when we mean "no" and "yes" when we mean "yes"

- Practice effective communication techniques

- Clear out negative residue daily

Prioritize Togetherness

If you and your partner are not connecting spontaneously and joyfully on a regular basis, schedule a block of hours each week for outings and for time together at home. Making dates in advance, unromantic as it may sound, ensures that individual concerns will not fall by the wayside—which can easily happen amid the day-to-day demands of early parenting.

During your together time, talk about the highlights and low points of your day, all the while sharing confidences. Discuss how parenthood is affecting you. Let each other in on what you were like as children, who your heroes and heroines are, and what your earlier relationships were like. Share previously untold tales of mischief, adventure, rebellion, and accomplishment.

Stay Up-to-Date on Expectations

Successful teamwork also hinges on sharing hopes and dreams for the future—reveries naturally awakened by new parenthood. If as a child you learned to keep your wishes and desires to yourself, coming out with them now can feel awkward and uncomfortable. Nevertheless, airing them is part of building a strong partnership. Why? Because unmet needs and desires that remain cloistered for too long take a toll on even the most committed relationships. An excellent preventative is to ask yourself two questions on an ongoing basis: "What do I want from my partner right now?" and "What am I willing (not willing) to give right now?"

Although it is best to begin discussing what you would like from each other well before your baby arrives, any time is better than never at all. If you feel uncomfortable asking your partner directly to do something for you, look inside and ask, "Where did I learn to hold back?" Of course, this behavior is another remnant from childhood. Take a moment to recall how your parents responded to your requests. Did they ignore you, put you down, divert your attention? Were you "guilt-tripped," told to stop being selfish, punished? Do you remember when you decided to stop asking? Although holding back was probably a wise decision at the time, circumstances are different now. Your partner is not your mother (father, grandparent, stepparent, or guardian). Your time with your partner is for living and loving, not merely coping and maintaining safety, as before. While respecting what *was*, have the wisdom to enjoy what *is*.

Holding back your wishes and desires—like other old, conditioned responses that block your happiness—will intrude on your intimacy. If you give your partner the chance to meet your expectations, she is sure to respond differently from anyone in your past. And to grow, you must face the unknown.

Imagine the Future

Casting a glance at the future together strongly enhances partnership solidarity. If you are pregnant now, spend time together imagining life with your newborn. What new demands will be placed on each of you? Who will feed, bathe, and dress the baby? Who will put her to bed, and who will get up with her in the middle of the night? Who will change and wash the diapers? Who will cook, clean, shop, and run errands? Who will be in charge of greeting visitors and fielding calls from relatives and friends? How much time off from work do you each want to take? Whose needs will take priority—yours, your partner's, your child's? When and how will you find time for yourself and each other?

If you are already ensconced in family life, sit down with your partner and imagine the tasks that might arise three months from now, then apportion them equitably. Wherever you are on the parenting continuum, put together a preliminary parenting agreement; you can always revise it as unforeseen responsibilities or new preferences arise. Collaborating on these important matters before facing them head-on will help launch your teamwork approach.

Agree to Disagree

There is a nasty rumor afoot that happy couples never fight or complain. Don't believe it. Not only is it unrealistic for you and your partner to expect agreement on all issues, but it would also prove boring and undesirable. Think of conflict as an energetic clash between two vibrant colors, perhaps fiery orange and dazzling purple. Then agree to disagree openly and fairly, and let your passions flow.

Allow for Time-Outs

Conflicts can and do get out of hand, especially when resentment has been building up and dialogue has reached an impasse. To guard against hurtfulness, agree to activate this contingency plan: Before a disagreement turns toxic, call a time-out. The protocol is simple—one person requests the time-out, then together you decide on meeting at a prearranged time and place to try again.

Hold "Clearing" Sessions

You may not always realize how upset you are or the storms that are brewing for your partner. To discourage an accumulation of anger and resentment, set aside time regularly for clearing your minds of disappointments, frustrations, and unhappiness of any kind. During these sessions, work with the following exercise.

FIGURE 10–4

Five Minutes of Free Speech

Think of this practice as a precaution against the buildup of volatile emotions.

- Spend five minutes saying everything you want to, knowing that your partner will not interrupt you. If getting started is difficult, fumble around until your feelings come into focus. (Five minutes is a lot of time, so don't feel rushed.) No topic is off limits; you may complain, ramble, or free associate to your heart's content provided that you use "I" statements all the way.

- Spend the next five minutes listening to your partner say everything that is on her mind. Remember, no interrupting. Just take it all in.

Amp Up Your Nonverbal Communication

Words often fail to convey the heart's message. At times they even refuse to surface. In such moments, nothing is as revealing as a warm smile, a loving touch, an understanding glance, an embrace, a lap to rest in, or a shoulder to cry on. Love speaks powerfully in silence.

Since nonverbal communication is such a potent medium for harmonious teamwork, take stock of when, where, and how you feel best being together without words—watching videos, perhaps, or listening to music, dancing, cuddling, working side by side, even tackling different projects in separate rooms. Create more of these precious moments, and decide never to abandon them.

Remember, too, that touch transcends words. When, where, and how do you enjoy touching and caressing each other? Give frequent massages. Let your fingers express your love. As the renowned anthropologist Ashley Montagu has said, "The healing power of touch is beyond our wildest dreams."[1]

11

What Our Children Really Need

My relationship with three-year-old Isaac is very much like my wife's. I have the same feelings about taking care of him, being with him, holding and playing with him. I thought only moms had that special kind of bond with their kids, but I do too, and it's great.

Although fathering is best begun while listening to our babies' heartbeats in utero, it is never too late to get involved and give our children what they really need. Father-child glue can start setting up at any time—while rocking our newborns; bathing with our infants; kneeling down to guide our toddlers' first steps; catching a smile meant just for us; backpacking, reading, dancing, or wrestling with our preschoolers; spending the morning in our first graders' classes; playing checkers or baseball with our fifth graders; or talking about dating with our teenagers.

Giving our children what they really need requires no advance knowledge, because fathering is not about doing it right. Instead, it is about being a loving dad—being available enough to hear what our children are saying, aware enough to learn from our past, confident enough to trust our instincts, and wise enough to respect the natural unfolding of our youngsters' lives. For this, you simply need to discover ways to be with your child. Ease into the search slowly. Anticipate uncertainty, ask questions, risk being wrong. And by all means, seize each opportunity you can to let your inner child out to play.

As years go by, you will begin shadowing your youngster. Sometimes you'll move smoothly and gracefully; at other times, you'll stumble. When you catch glimpses of your own childhood, allow the memories to flow. Gliding back and forth between your child's experiences and your own helps you "grok" what he is grappling with.

My friend Howard recently told me he saw his eight-year-old son, Ian, in his old 1960s Cub Scout uniform. Instantly, Howard flashed back to his elementary school days. His first memories were of being painfully shy and self-conscious. As more memories emerged, his face took on a childlike glow, and he recounted the camaraderie he felt with his Cub Scout troop. Suddenly, Howard knew just what his son needed from him. He put his arm around Ian and said, "I'll go to the Scout meeting with you. Hey, did I ever tell you about my days in the Scouts?"

Swimming in the ocean with his six-year-old daughter cast Eli back in time to summers with his mother at the Jersey shore. Feeling a bit shaky, Eli recalled his childhood dread of the ocean. Then his discomfort lifted as he remembered how buoyant he felt when his mother slipped her hands beneath him in the water, supporting his body and teaching him to float. Instinctively, Eli stretched out his arms to prop up his daughter as the next wave rolled in.

When my son Jesse started playing organized basketball, I

watched him dash up and down the court panting, straining to keep up. When he missed a pass or double-dribbled, I prayed he wouldn't be too discouraged. When he made an assist or a sweet swish, I hoped he wouldn't get cocky. I was glued to his every move and each new expression on his face. I had been there myself so many times, bombarded by the gripping emotions that initiate boys into the rigors of male competition.

There are endless ways to be with our children, and each one teaches us something new. Eye to eye with them, we come to see the world as they do. Listening to their insights, giggles, and sobs, we gain perspective on our own lives. Tapping into the full range of our power, we learn to open up, exercise our many gifts, and cultivate new abilities as well. Before long, we wake up to the startling realization that fathering is a major event on the playing field of personal growth, and that by giving it our all we move toward greater wisdom and wholeness.

AN OPEN BOOK OR AN OPEN HEART?

Over the past decade, a plethora of parenting books has flooded the market. A quick trip to your favorite bookstore, online or off, will reveal every formula imaginable. Pick the type of child you might want and there's a title or two for you. A recent Internet search brought up volumes that promised to help me raise the child of my dreams—a kid who is happy and secure; confident and self-sufficient; kind, responsible, and well-mannered; healthy, good-hearted, and spirited; bright, talented, capable, and drug-free . . . even money-wise. (I get nervous just thinking of all the subjects I must not know enough about!)

The truth is that effective fathering does not require an instruction manual of any sort; instead, it calls for strong character and a loving attitude. Children do not need the latest in child-rearing techniques. They need parents who know themselves and each other, and who understand that parenting is a spiritual endeavor sustained by love and nurturing.

After all, children's identities are shaped by the people in their world. And their sense of self is fostered by the reflections they see in the faces around them. In this sense, we are our children's first mirrors. Our attention and approval, our smiles, and our hugs let them know that they are cherished and valuable.

We can best guide the course of our children's growth by meeting their essential needs, as is illustrated in figure 11–1. When we approach this task with a joyful sense of responsibility, we come to the marvelous realization that *we have everything it takes to fulfill our children's needs.* All we have to do is open our hearts and step out of the way.

FIGURE 11–1

Meeting Your Child's Twelve Essential Needs

Need	How to Meet It
For connection (a sense of belonging)	Express acceptance, appreciation, and love directly and openly. • Spend one-on-one time each day with your child. • Hug, cuddle, and lie down together. • Talk to each other about day-to-day events and dreams. • Greet your child warmly each day. • Play, shop, work, and eat together. • Continually remind your child of the special place he holds in your family history. • Take family photos (with you included). • Massage your child.

For support	Show interest in your child's interests.
	• Build and feather the nest.
	• Work together on your child's pet projects.
	• Encourage patience, hard work, and self-reliance.
	• Emphasize effort over results.
	• Accentuate personal satisfaction over approval from others.
	• Describe what makes your child special to you.
	• Share personal anecdotes that parallel your child's experiences so that he will not feel unusual or alone.
For protection	Shield your child from needless physical, emotional, or spiritual injury.
	• Set limits based on safety and logical consequences.
	• Welcome your child's requests for help.
	• Tell your child what you are experiencing; otherwise, he may be prompted to internalize your moods, make assumptions, or become a mind reader.
	• Never threaten your child with rejection or abandonment. Differentiate between disapproving of his behavior and disapproving of his inner self.
For freedom to explore	Encourage curiosity, reasonable risk taking, and attempts at self-mastery.
	• Invite imaginative thinking.

- Respect your child's opinions, choices, feelings, likes, and dislikes.
- Create opportunities for discovery, fun, and laughter together.
- Allow your child the full spectrum of feelings.
- Welcome your child's displays of affection.

For acceptance	Give your child frequent undivided attention and loving eye contact.

- Mirror your newborn's facial expressions, sounds, and movements.
- Actively listen to your child.
- Identify with your child's feelings by drawing upon your own.
- Show appreciation for your child every day.
- Spend time together doing what your child wants to do.
- Scratch each other's backs, wrestle, read, watch a special show, go to the movies, or just "hang out" together.
- Include your child in your favorite activities.
- Take your child to work with you.

For consistency	Be someone your child can count on no matter what.

- Provide reasonable consequences for misbehavior, and follow through on them.
- Model reliability.

	• Say what you mean and mean what you say.
	• Walk the walk; don't just talk it.
For flexibility	Be receptive to new ideas and differences of opinion.
	• Avoid getting locked in on being correct.
	• Don't keep score.
	• Check out your assumptions.
	• Give your child choices whenever possible.
	• Model open-mindedness and an appreciation for differences.
For self-awareness	Foster introspection.
	• Understand where you're coming from.
	• Take time getting to know yourself.
	• Tend to your unfinished business.
	• Take responsibility for meeting your needs, rather than expecting others to and blaming them when they don't.
	• Nurture yourself, and deepen your enjoyment of life.
	• Share your spiritual beliefs with your child, and encourage him to discover his own seeds of faith.
	• Inquire about your child's experiences and feelings.
For self-expression	Allow for the full range of emotional expression as long as it causes no injury to people or property.

- Demonstrate your love openly, in words and deeds.
- Be real—show your enthusiasm and discouragement.
- Emphasize creativity over success, process over accomplishment.
- Hold family meetings to clear feelings.
- Resolve disagreements before bedtime.

For fair treatment Give your child the benefit of the doubt.
- Be considerate; avoid judging.
- Include your child in rule making, decision making, and planning.
- Set limits, enforce appropriate consequences, and be willing to discuss them.
- Own up to your mistakes.
- Apologize for hurting others' feelings, even when you think you are right.

For socialization Let be, and gradually let go.
- Introduce your child to caring adults in the community.
- Don't take your child's criticism and rejection personally; see them as signs of his struggle toward independence.
- Teach cooperation.
- Welcome your child's friends into your home and your heart.
- Volunteer in the community.

	• Attempt to improve relations with your ex, if only for your child's sake.
	• Encourage group dating.
For empowerment	Model firmness and assertiveness, vulnerability and resourcefulness.
	• Focus on what's right, not what's wrong.
	• Don't overanticipate your child's requests.
	• Offer reassurance that your child's feelings and behaviors are "normal."
	• Listen, accept, and guide, rather than preach, judge, or criticize.
	• Encourage self-reliance.

A FATHER'S TOUCH

Although rarely addressed in the popular literature, children also need ongoing exposure to a father's firm, tender, and loving touch. Research in human development confirms what we have known intuitively all along—that frequent, nurturing touch is essential for healthy development and the formation of close relationships. Moreover, as Ashley Montagu has suggested, "If, in our culture, we could learn to understand the importance of fathers as well as mothers giving their infants adequate touch, we would be taking a considerable step toward the improvement of human relations."[1]

To thrive in every way possible, our children need us to hold them, carry them, caress them, and cuddle them. In fact, our touch is more life-enhancing than any wisdom we may pass on to them. By cultivating the art of loving touch in all its wonderful variations—stroking, rocking, rubbing, gentle scratching, tickling, soothing, massaging—we are most likely to ensure that our children will flourish.

The Gifts of Touch

We are only now learning about the enormous benefits of touch throughout the early stages of human development. As you will see, however, an important chunk of this information remains "classified."

To track it down, let's start at the beginning as we know it. We are introduced to the world through the warm, embracing tissues of our mother's body. Our first contact with others is through the hands that lift us out of the birth canal and into the arms of one of our parents. To this day we carry a memory of that touch in our unconscious.

And so it is for our children. In the very beginning, even in utero, touch forms the conduit through which our children experience safety. Touch also lets our infants know that they belong, that they are lovable. Close body contact—hugging, patting, caressing, soothing—calms them as well, and restores their equilibrium.

Gradually, as our children grow, our voices take the place of touch. Gentle words spoken in reassuring tones remind them of a warm embrace. And a scolding delivered in angry tones makes them cry, as if we had hit them.

During latency, our boys and girls typically seek less physical contact with us. Through body language, if nothing else, they let us know whether or not they want to be touched. Eight-year-old Daniel, however, came right out and told his father that he no longer wanted to be hugged in public.

> Daniel told me he didn't want to be hugged goodbye when I dropped him off at school. He did say it was okay to hug him at home but not when his friends were around. I couldn't believe he had put so much thought into this "hugging bit." I have mixed feelings about it—I'm proud that he knows his own mind and sad that I've got to back away now.

At puberty, our children's need for touch resurfaces, often peaking in response to the stresses of adolescence. In satisfying this renewed need for touch, we help fulfill our teens' quests for intimacy and acceptance.

The top-secret aspect of touch is this: Children who have drawn safety, comfort, reassurance, and security from our touch will offer the same gifts to their children. Touch, in other words, is *a precious legacy we pass on to future generations*.

The Hands-Off Compromise

If a father's touch reverberates down through the generations, why don't we all scoop up our newborns in our arms, kiss their faces, and draw them toward our chests? Is it because we believe mother's breast is a baby's ultimate comfort zone? Do we fail to recognize that our bodies serve infants equally well? Or is it that we are uncomfortable displaying affection to our children?

If you are among the large percentage of fathers who adhere to a "hands-off" parenting policy, chances are that you feel ill at ease displaying affection openly to your child. To find out for sure, examine your attitude toward touching in general. How do you react to being touched, to touching others, to saying or being told, "I love you"?

Now consider how these reactions color your relationship with your child. How comfortable are you holding your child close? Kissing him? Stroking and comforting him? Holding his hand? Lying skin-to-skin and hugging him? When you read that your child needs all the loving touch you can give him, what feelings stir within you?

It is safe to assume that your present attitude toward displays of affection is an outgrowth of your earliest experiences with touch. What do you remember of your childhood contact with your mom? With your dad? Did they touch you? If so, how? When? How frequently? What memories do you have of them as affectionate adults? What messages did they convey, overtly or covertly, about touching others? Touching yourself? About giving and receiving pleasure through skin-to-skin contact?

Think specifically of your father. Did you *feel* his love for you?

How did he show it? Did he hold you close, lie next to you, pat your head, rub or scratch it? Did he hold your hand, put his arm around your shoulder, cup your face? Or did he show affection from a distance, slapping your back, shaking your hand, or "giving you five"—or keep you at bay with stern words, silence, moodiness, or punishment? Or was there no meaningful contact between you at all?

If you received adequate physical tenderness from your father, expressing affection toward your own child is likely to come instinctively. If you were deprived of your father's loving touch, displaying affection for your child may be difficult. And you have most likely found ways to cover your losses. When confronted, you may explain that being physical just isn't your way. Or you may limit body contact to the sports arena or the bedroom.

For men deprived of a father's touch, maneuvers such as these only obscure the discomfort we feel when we get close to others. As a result, they do not help us become the fathers our children need. To grow, we must come to terms with our early losses and learn to take pleasure in displays of affection and intimacy.

Warming Up to Touch

Most any discomfort you feel with physical closeness can be overcome. First, recognize that your inhibitions did not arise "out of the blue," are not unique to you, and do not signify a personal deficit or character flaw. Rather, they are embedded in our social conditioning.

In most Western cultures boys, unlike girls, are expected to pull away from their mothers, ready or not, at a relatively early age to attach to their fathers. Notwithstanding the cultural imperative to leave mom or be overfeminized, boys feel a powerful pull toward their dads—an urge to connect with them in a primary, male way. Poet Robert Bly portrays a memorable picture of what happens when a father and son are able to establish this bond:

> When a father and son spend long hours together
> . . . a substance almost like food passes from the
> older body to the younger, at a level far below

consciousness. His cells receive some knowledge of what an adult masculine body is...at what frequency the masculine body vibrates, to grasp the song that adult male cells sing. A circle is completed.[2]

Most of us have never experienced anything resembling this type of relationship with our dads. We knew mostly wounded men who were unavailable and ill prepared for fathering, overworked, overwhelmed with responsibilities, and often secretly depressed. As a result, far too many of us felt doubly deprived— missing the deep connection with our mothers and lacking the physical affection we craved with our fathers.

Moreover, we assumed that the failure to connect with our fathers was our fault. We brooded in silence, wondering, "What's wrong with me? Why doesn't Dad spend time with me, play with me, wrestle with me, hug and kiss me?" We had no idea that the disconnect with our fathers had nothing to do with us—that the shame and emptiness we carried around emanated from a hole in our fathers' psyches.

Seeking desperately to alleviate the pain of our fathers' rejection, we set out to win their approval, to secure their interest in us at whatever cost. We worked hard to meet their expectations, to be good sons in their eyes. Eventually feeling defeated, hurt, and angry without understanding why, we pushed away—denying the importance of our fathers' love and approval, only to unconsciously act out our unfulfilled emotional needs in other relationships.

What other recourse did we have? Going back to mom would have meant regression and humiliation. Getting more from dad was seemingly impossible. And discussion was impractical: These existential dilemmas were not the sorts of problems we could, or would, have talked about.

As years passed, we remained silent and out of touch with both our pain and our desire for physical tenderness. Why? Because the duck-and-hide, suppress-and-succeed prescriptions our macho culture offered us never addressed the pain of our unrequited longing for a father's love. Witness today's male sports heroes, many raised exclusively by their mothers, as they greet television cameras with smiles and calls of "Hi, Mom. I love you!" How often do they wave at their dads and thank them for being there? Regrettably, we have all been trained to compete—on playing fields and battlefields, in ghettos, factories, and corporate offices—without crying out (or even speaking up) for what we need most from those who most need us.

The good news is that fatherhood is not about competition or success or "toughing it out." On the contrary, it offers us unlimited opportunities to be real, and to be for our children what we secretly wanted for ourselves—a fully present, demonstratively loving dad who willingly transmits his love through the magic of touch.

For now, picture some of these opportunities in your mind. Then little by little, release your inhibitions and warm up to touch. During pregnancy, gently caress the rounded abdomen that shelters your baby-to-be, sending love through your fingertips. As you do, imagine him receiving a stream of tenderness and caring. Keep this practice going on a steady basis and you will be primed for hands-on fathering as soon as your baby emerges.

The Art of Infant Massage

A father's touch performs its magic powerfully through infant massage—an easy, natural, and mutually rewarding way to father right from the start. Massaging our babies results in a win-win-win outcome. Our babies win by reaping a host of psychosocial and physiological rewards. We win by developing latent sensitivities and renewed confidence. In fact, dads whose partners are breast-feeding are often delighted to learn that the hormonal effects produced during skin-to-skin contact are the same as those produced during nipple stimulation, suggesting that through ongoing infant massage a father can attach deeply to his baby. A diagram showing specific benefits to babies and massage givers, all of which have been well researched, appears in figure 11–2.

FIGURE 11–2

The Benefits of Infant Massage[3]

Psychosocial benefits to our infants

- Promotes bonding and attachment
- Deepens the body-mind-spirit connection
- Increases self-esteem
- Fosters a sense of love, acceptance, respect, and trust
- Enhances communication

Physiological benefits to our infants

- Improves body awareness
- Encourages relaxation and release of accumulated stress
- Stimulates circulation
- Strengthens digestive, circulatory, and gastrointestinal systems, which can lead to weight gain
- Reduces discomfort from teething, congestion, gas, colic, and emotional stress
- Increases muscle tone and coordination
- Enhances elimination, circulation, and respiration
- Improves sleep patterns
- Activates hormonal functions

Benefits to us, the massage-givers

- Improves ability to read infant cues
- Increases synchrony between caregiver and infant
- Promotes bonding
- Increases confidence in parenting
- Inspires communication—verbal and nonverbal

- Improves relaxation
- Provides uninterrupted one-on-one time together
- Promotes implementation of parenting skills
- Improves sense of well-being
- Reduces blood pressure
- Reduces stress
- Improves overall health

The third winner in the introduction of infant massage is the father-child relationship. Infants, as we know, communicate through their bodies. When you engage your infant in a massage, you begin to listen to sounds, you watch and feel movements, you "listen" with your eyes, your ears, your hands, and your heart. Touch communication nurtures the most important relationship your child will ever have. Getting to know your child through touch, you begin to form a lifelong heartfelt bond with him—all in the relaxing environment of your home. As Chris, a father of three, puts it:

> When I do quiet stuff with my kids—reading, crafts, or watching movies—or even active things like soccer or catch, my head can be off somewhere else. But when I massage my kids, I'm there 1,000 percent. The feedback I get, without a word uttered, is terrific: "You make me feel good, Dad." It's like the old Sonny and Cher song that goes, "You've got me and, baby, I've got you." There's nothing quite like it.

Infant massage can be started on day one if your baby weighs at least six pounds, and it may be continued daily. The techniques themselves are best learned in group or private sessions with a

Certified Infant Massage Instructor, although books are also helpful (see Suggested Reading at the back of the book). Here are
some pertinent points:

- Massaging your baby is harmless and goof-proof. There is no
  "wrong" way to massage a baby.
- Babies like gentle but firm touch. Pressure feels good to them;
  touch that is hesitant or too light is unpleasant and unlikely to
  yield positive effects.
- For best results, massage your baby's stomach in a clockwise
  direction.
- Proceed slowly and patiently. It may take a week or two for your
  baby (and you) to feel at ease with massage.
- Take time off from massage whenever your baby has a fever.

Our children's arrival inaugurates us into parenthood. And
before we can catch our breath, we are swept up by the com-
pelling physiological and psychological forces churning within
them. Each new stage of growth reverberates with struggles we
can recall from our own youth, awakening us to the importance
of fulfilling their childhood needs. Then as our sons and daughters approach maturity still reaching out to us, we begin to wonder if parenthood will ever end. Sooner or later, the wise father
recognizes that it indeed lasts forever—that even as an adult his
child's essential needs endure, as do his own needs for love, acceptance, and closeness.

12

Fathering through the Stages

*For weeks after they were born I held my kids in my
lap. [So much] starts in the lap: bouncing, sleeping, sitting, climbing . . . hanging, resting, diaper changing, and
all this time, touching. In holding is delight. . . . The lap
is always there, secure acreage, so eventually kids
branch off to explore the world. Over the years the
exploring only gets more complex.*
                                        —Patch Adams

Infancy propels our children toward toddlerhood,
early childhood toward adolescence, and puberty
toward young adulthood. As nature would have it, there is mag-
nificent order and purpose in this master plan. While parenting
our children through the twists and turns of each new stage of
growth, we discover that their needs remain fundamentally the
same and that the secret to artful parenting is to strive ever harder

to meet them. Stretching each step of the way to support our children's unfolding maturation, we ourselves are transformed over and over again, increasing our self-knowledge and opening us more fully to the inevitability of change. The wonder and glory of it all is that in supporting our children's development, we grow right along with them.

INFANCY AND TODDLERHOOD: FROM BREAST TO CHEST

Your partner, who by nature's design provides the initial nutrients for your infant's growth and immunity, is her primary attachment figure. As a father, you come in second. Keep in mind, however, that you are by no means second string.

Having played this "odd man out" role in a previous mother-child breastfeeding ritual, I promised myself that the second time around, things would be different. I would not be the man-in-waiting hanging in the wings again. My only question was, how could it be otherwise?

Toward the end of pregnancy, I shared my wishes for increased participation with my wife, Ellen. To my delight, she was receptive. We agreed to form a breastfeeding trio: at nursing time, all three of us would nestle up together. And we did—while Jesse breastfed, I either placed my hand on his belly or Ellen's, or simply relaxed with them, daydreaming, talking quietly, or singing.

I reveled in being part of this trio. Weeks after his birth, Jesse, by then very familiar with my voice and touch, began turning toward me after nursing. As more time passed, he started to look at me and reach for me, first with his hand or leg, and later with his entire body. I, in turn, would carefully position him on my chest and gently rock him off to sleep.

Whether or not you form your own breastfeeding trio, be sure to build in lots of chest-to-chest contact and lap time with your little one. Heartbeat to heartbeat and chest to chest, you will fall in love with each other.

Before long, your child will be a toddler and you will be her male link to the world. Through you, she will come to know masculine realities—the rough-and-tumble, push-and-pull of male play; the strong and guiding, yet gentle touch of a man; and an action-oriented approach to situations. You will probably be the one to say, "Try it," "Check it out," "Go for it," "Don't be afraid," "I bet you can do it," and "I'm watching." Your encouragement will support your toddler's natural curiosity and striving for mastery and independence. Finding security with dad is a surefire way to learn that life is navigable, that it is safe to venture away from the protective envelope of mom and home, and that others can be trusted.

THE SCHOOL-AGE YEARS

Children venturing off to school must contend with a myriad of social forces, including acceptance, cooperation, sharing, and competition. Their primary tasks are to learn how to engage others, how to get their own social and emotional needs met, and how to behave as boys and girls within a cultural context.

Leaving the hearth is the first leg of the critically important psychosocial process called "individuation," which ultimately leads a child toward an understanding of her unique identity and personal destiny. The drive to individuate carries children from almost total dependency on their parents into the community, where self-knowledge, autonomy, and interdependency begin to flourish. While testing the waters of individuation, however, children are pulled by an equally powerful wish to remain attached to the safety of home. These conflicting drives often manifest in periodic bouts of frustration, fear, anxiety, anger, and resentment, as they did for Jason, much to his father's exasperation.

I never know from one day to the next whether or not Jason will give me a hard time getting off to school. Sometimes he's clingy, and at other times he seems happy as a clam to go. So I've come up with a few strategies: asking him what he's thinking or feeling, giving lots of hugs and reassurance, and just trying to get an earlier start in the mornings. Some days these tactics work better than others. . . . It'll sure be nice when he outgrows this behavior and stops testing my patience.

To assist your child through this developmental dilemma, draw on childhood memories of your own search for identity, including power struggles with your parents. The more you can recapture the inner experience of testing limits, rebelling, and defying authority, or of complying and turning passively inward, the easier it will be to appreciate your child's emotional predicament.

Also encourage your youngster to discharge frustrations by running, yelling, jumping, kicking a ball, or hitting a punching bag. Have her talk out her feelings as well, and express them through writing, painting, crafts, music, or dance. Teach her the value of bringing levity and laughter to difficult situations. Most of all, let her know you are always there by her side.

While interacting with you, your child assimilates your values. For instance, the way you spend leisure time—alone or with friends, at home or in the community, working or playing, thinking or doing, preoccupied or available—shapes her view of what's important. To model life-affirming principles as she reaches for self-understanding, mastery, and maturity, extend your borders right along with her. Limber up by asking yourself these questions:

- What is my relationship with my body, my senses, and my spirit? Do I exercise, rest, dance, sing? Do I meditate, pray, rejoice? Am I grateful? Am I joyful?
- What is my relationship to nature? Do I garden, hike, ride, climb, surf? Do I show appreciation for nature? Am I connected

to the earth? Do I conserve resources as well as consume them?

- How do I participate in my community? Am I involved in my child's education, sports activities, artistic pursuits, religious school? Do I take part in neighborhood or civic projects? Do I get together with other men who support the well-being of children?

If stretching in the direction of other fathers is of interest to you, recognize that more and more dads are eager to "talk fathering." You can find them almost anywhere—at the local YMCA, at soccer games, at churches and synagogues, in public libraries, in traditional men's clubs, at school open houses, and on class trips. Casual settings, such as parks, cafes, juice bars, ice cream parlors, and backyards are also conducive to conversations about parenting.

ADOLESCENCE: EN ROUTE TO AUTONOMY

Adolescents have entered the next leg of the trek to individuation. Encumbered with the day-to-day challenges of high school and all that comes next—jobs, college, marriage, and career—they are struggling to separate from us while frantically sorting out their ambivalence about growing up.

It's time to fasten your seat belt, for you are sure to be drawn into the turmoil. Why? Because you are a natural target—someone for your teenager to push up against, defy, blame, and rebel against. James was visibly annoyed while describing the antics of his teenage daughter:

> Things were good till she hit age thirteen or fourteen—maybe too good. Then suddenly those hormones kicked in, and now, instead of wanting to read together or cuddle or talk. . . . Well, let's just say I'm glad when she's out with her friends. I've decided that parenting a teenager is nothing short of a trial by fire.

Adolescence introduces that dreaded period, much more trying than the "testy twos" and far more protracted and painful, when parents feel under attack and begin counting the days till Junior or Sweet Pea leaves home, evacuating the nest for parts unknown. Instead of taking these assaults personally and turning defensive or aggressive yourself, let the harsh words and provocative behavior roll off your back. Then set your telephoto lens on the big picture: Beneath your child's toughness and anger is acute sensitivity, a heightened fear of rejection from friends, and occasionally overwhelming confusion about the best directions to take.

Why do teenagers direct their frustrations at their parents? Because it is their job as individuators to strike out, and they know it is safer to be angry with us than with anyone else. Lashing out at others, they risk being ostracized, rejected, or abandoned. With us, they can count on continued caring. We are our children's life nets. We must remain steadfastly in place for them even when we disapprove of their actions or resent their attitudes. This is *our* job as responsible, loving parents.

If you grew up without the security of an emotional life net, your task will be extra challenging. Bruised by a parent's insensitivity, negligence, or abusiveness, you are most likely programmed to repeat similar patterns, especially when your adolescent pushes your buttons. Although you may have vowed never to reenact the yelling, hitting, sarcasm, or criticism of your parents, remember that for better and for worse, there is some of mom and dad in each of us.

The solution is not to blame your parents or yourself, or to deny the hurt, irritation, or anger you may feel toward your teenager. Rather, it is to elevate your self-awareness and to refrain from acting impulsively. Recognize that because you were mistreated as a child, you must work especially hard to maintain healthy communication with your own child.

Any time you catch yourself playing out a negative scene from your past, stop in your tracks and switch off the "automatic pilot." Then set both hands on the wheel and take a good hard look at the rebellious teenager within you. Question the value in continuing this family legacy. Commit to erasing the unhealthy patterns you learned and to constructing a new family dynamic. Be patient with yourself, and push onward. The rewards will be immeasurable.

NURTURING MATTERS

Dr. Sandor Ferenczi, a disciple of Freud's, was once asked to name the curative elements underlying psychotherapy. He replied that the true healing power is love. The art of effective therapy, he added, is in offering the unique kind of love each individual most needs.

So it is with effective fathering. A good father strives to give each of his children the love that meets their changing needs. Depending on a child's stage of development, there are times for comforting and for confronting, for speaking out and for listening, for flexibility and for firmness, for letting go and for drawing near.

The medium for conveying these rich and varied expressions of father-love is *nurturance*. What does nurturance encompass? It spans the entire range of behaviors described in previous chapters: connecting, touching, hugging, kissing, stroking, back scratching, cuddling, caretaking, exploring, teaching, affectionate communication, support, encouragement, reinforcement, personal sharing, constructive feedback, accessibility, and attentiveness.

As we know, nurturing tops today's list of cultural expectations for fathers. However, despite our expectation that dads express more caring and affection than ever before, male nurturing behaviors are under scrutiny. Some people claim that these behaviors can foster an unhealthy dependency in children, weakening their character. Others are concerned that a father's nurturing behaviors may compromise his authority over his children. Still others question whether a father who is "too affectionate" might undermine his son's gender development, leaving him confused and susceptible to homosexuality, or interfere with a daughter's psychological development.

Fortunately, a growing number of studies unequivocally refute these notions. Here are some welcome findings:

- Nurturing fathers inspire competence, independence, and self-reliance in their children. Nurturing provides fertile soil in which emotional security, self-esteem, self-confidence, and autonomy are able to take root and flourish.
- Fathers who are less emotionally involved with their children resort more often to arbitrary and ineffective disciplinary techniques.
- Children with nurturing fathers are more generous, empathetic, altruistic, tolerant, and understanding than those with relatively uninvolved fathers.
- Nurturing fathers inspire their sons to be like them, thereby helping to secure gender identity. Boys who are nurtured by their fathers come to value their own nurturing capacities as integral to their masculinity.
- Nurturing fathers provide their daughters with a firm basis for feeling accepted, valued, and effective as women; a solid foundation for weathering early insecurities in relationships; and a model for choosing men who will treat them with respect. Further, women who are close to their fathers during childhood, compared with those who are not, go on to engage in more fulfilling heterosexual relationships.

As your son's dad, you have the awesome distinction of being his first male role model. If you feel "squared away" with yourself as a man, passing on your values and ways becomes a special gift for both of you; however, if you are struggling to feel more successful or complete as a man, raising a son may feel like a mixed blessing. A good dad supports his son's *efforts* more than his *accomplishments*. He tells his son about growing up male as he knew it, positioning himself as a valued friend as well as a figurehead. He strives to be clear, consistent, and unconditionally available. He welcomes his son's friendships with others, allowing always for the all-important pursuit of autonomy and self-mastery. And in honoring his relationship with his partner, a good dad teaches his son, in words and deeds, how to treat women with respect, appreciation, and equality.

As the first man in your daughter's life, you have the honor of being her premier male coach. A good coach will cheer his daughter on whether she is on an athletic field, in a spelling bee, or part of a theatrical production. If and when your daughter becomes seriously interested in dating, let her know what respectful boys find attractive in girls. Help her set standards for everyone she interacts with, adults as well as peers. Encourage her to follow her interests, assert herself, and avoid giving her power away. Teach her the importance of saying "no" and of protecting herself physically when necessary. Set high expectations so that she will rise to the challenge of meeting them. You'll be amazed at the far-reaching effects of your efforts.

We contain within us all the ingredients needed for raising healthy, competent children who are not afraid to live up to their potential. But to bring this desire to fruition, we too must be courageous. Moving intrepidly through whatever fears distance us from loved ones, we can become the generation of men that gives its children the gift of involved, demonstrative, nurturing dads.

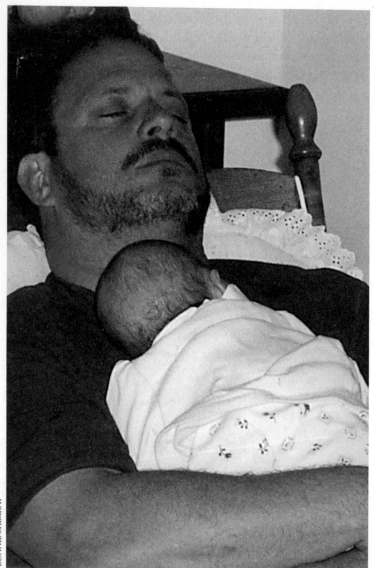

Epilogue

In our hearts we know that fathering is about being men, in the richest and noblest sense of the word. We know, too, that our image of masculinity was fractured and we have been ailing. Our gut tells us that being a man has nothing to do with conquering, winning, proving, being strong, being right, or being good; instead, it means being fully ourselves, loving and caring with others, and welcoming their affection for us. Fathering is essentially about discovering and learning, stretching and maturing, finding meaning and purpose, and going beyond ourselves rather than merely providing. To be a dad we and our children are proud of therefore requires soul-searching, tenacity, commitment, and courage. And we are up to the task.

Start now to grow into fathering. Love and nurture your child whenever you can, in whatever ways feel right for you. When your deepest instincts tell you to embrace your crying son, to kiss your daughter's forehead and stroke her hair, to be moved by your toddler's joy and pain, to lie quietly beside your adolescent and thank God for the wonder of creation, do it.

Say "yes" to fathering, right from the start.

Notes

Introduction

1. The National Fatherhood Initiative, *Fatherhood and TV* (March 1999): p. 2–3.
2. Patricia Cohen, "Daddy Dearest: Do You Really Matter?" *New York Times* (11 July 1998): pp. A–1 and A–15.
3. David Blankenhorn, *Fatherless in America: Confronting Our Most Urgent Social Problem* (New York: Basic Books, 1995), p. 3.

Chapter 1

1. Dan Kindlon and Michael Thompson, *Raising Cain: Protecting the Emotional Life of Boys* (New York: Ballantine Books, 1999), p. 100.
2. Ibid.
3. Sam Keen, *Fire in the Belly: On Being a Man* (New York: Bantam, 1991), pp. 47–48.
4. Ibid., p. 48.

Chapter 8

1. James Hillman, *Fathers and Mothers* (Dallas, TX: Spring Publications, 1990), p. 36.
2. Terrence Real, *I Don't Want to Talk about It: Overcoming the Secret Legacy of Male Depression* (New York: Simon & Schuster, 1998), p. 35.
3. Ibid., p. 63.

Chapter 10

1. Ashley Montagu, *Touching: The Human Significance of the Skin* (New York: Harper & Row, 1972), p. 126.

Chapter 11

1. Ashley Montagu, *Touching: The Human Significance of the Skin* (New York: Harper & Row, 1972), p. 314.
2. Robert Bly, *Iron John: A Book about Men* (Reading, MA: Addison-Wesley, 1990), p. 93.
3. Compiled from research presented in Elaine Fogel Schneider's "Touch Communication: The Power of Infant Massage," a Web site article (Sonoma, CA: Foundation for Healthy Family Living, 1999).

Suggested Reading

PREGNANCY

Arms, Suzanne. *Seasons of Change: Growing through Pregnancy and Birth*. Durango, CO: Kaviki, 1993.

Bing, Elisabeth, and Libby Colman. *Making Love during Pregnancy*. New York: Bantam Books, 1977.

Bradford, Nikki. *The Miraculous World of Your Unborn Baby: A Week-by-Week Guide to Your Pregnancy*. Chicago: Contemporary Books, 1998.

Brazelton, Berry T. *On Becoming a Family: The Growth of Attachment before and after Birth*. New York: Delacorte Press, 1992.

Brenner, Paul. *Life Is a Shared Creation*. Marina del Rey, CA: DeVorss, 1981.

Brott, Armin A. *The Expectant Father: Facts, Tips, and Advice for Dads-to-Be*. New York: Abbeville Press. 1995.

Colman, Arthur, and Libby Colman. *Pregnancy: The Psychological Experience*. New York: The Seabury Press, 1973.

Eisenberg, Arlene, Heidi Murkoff, and Sandee Eisenberg. *What to Expect When You're Expecting*. New York: Workman Press, 1996.

Heinowitz, Jack. *Pregnant Fathers: Entering Parenthood Together*. San Diego, CA: Parents As Partners Press, 1995.

Hotchner, Tracy. *Pregnancy and Childbirth: The Complete Guide for a New Life.* New York: Avon, 1984.

Huxley, Laura, and Piero Ferrucci. *The Child of Your Dreams: Approaching Conception and Pregnancy with Inner Peace.* Rochester, VT: Destiny Books, 1992.

Mamie, Eve. *Love Start: Pre-birth Bonding.* Santa Monica, CA: Hay House, 1989.

Peterson, Gayle, and Lewis Mehl. *Pregnancy As Healing: A Holistic Philosophy for Prenatal Care.* Berkeley, CA: Mindbody Press, 1974.

Schwartz, Leni. *Bonding before Birth.* Boston: Sigo Press, 1991.

Verny, Thomas, with John Kelly. *The Secret Life of the Unborn Child.* New York: Delacorte Press, 1986.

Verny, Thomas, and Pamela Weintraub. *Nurturing the Unborn Child: A Nine-Month Program for Soothing, Stimulating, and Communicating with Your Baby.* New York: Delacorte Press, 1991.

Welwood, John. *Challenge of the Heart: Love, Sex, and Intimacy in Changing Times.* Boston: Shambhala, 1985.

BIRTH

Anderson, Sandra VanDam, and Penny Simkin. *Birth through Children's Eyes.* Seattle, WA: Pennypress, 1981.

Arms, Suzanne. *Immaculate Deception II: Myth, Magic and Birth.* Berkeley, CA: Celestial Arts, 1997.

Baldwin, Rahima. *Special Delivery.* Berkeley, CA: Celestial Arts, 1990.

Bowlby, John. *Attachment.* New York: Basic Books, 1992.

Bradley, Robert A. *Husband-Coached Childbirth.* New York: Harper & Row, 1965.

Capacchione, Lucia, and Sandra Bardsley. *Creating a Joyful Birth Experience.* New York: Simon & Schuster, 1994.

England, Pam, and Rob Horowitz. *Birthing from Within: An Extra-Ordinary Guide to Childbirth Preparation.* Albuquerque, NM: Partera Press, 1998.

English, Jane. *Different Doorway: Adventures of a Caesarean Born*. Mt. Shasta, CA: Earth Heart, 1985.

Harper, Barbara. *Gentle Birth Choices: A Guide to Making Informed Decisions*. Rochester, NY: Inner Traditions, 1994.

Jones, Carl. *Mind over Labor*. New York: Viking/Penguin, 1987.

Kitzinger, Sheila. *Giving Birth: The Parents' Emotions in Childbirth*. New York: Taplinger, 1971.

———. *Your Baby, Your Way: Making Pregnancy Decisions and Birth Plans*. New York: Pantheon, 1987.

Klaus, Marshall, John Kennell, and Phyllis Klaus. *Mothering the Mother: How a Doula Can Help You Have a Shorter, Easier, and Healthier Birth*. Reading, MA: Addison-Wesley, 1993.

Odent, Michel. *Birth Reborn*. New York: Pantheon, 1984.

Peterson, Gayle. *An Easier Childbirth: A Mother's Guide for Birthing Normally*. Berkeley, CA: Shadow & Light Publications, 1993.

Ray, Sondra, and Bob Mandel. *Birth and Relationships: How Your Birth Affects Your Relationships*. Berkeley, CA: Celestial Arts, 1987.

Zimmer, Judith. *Labor of Love: Mothers Share the Joy of Childbirth*. New York: John Wiley & Sons, 1997.

BEYOND

Anderson, Robert. *I Never Sang for My Father*. New York: Random House, 1966.

Bassoff, Evelyn S. *Between Mothers and Sons: The Making of Vital and Loving Men*. New York: Penguin Books, 1994.

Bing, Elizabeth, and Libby Colman. *Laughter and Tears: The Emotional Life of New Mothers*. New York: Henry Holt and Co., 1997.

Bradshaw, John. *The Family: A Revolutionary Way of Self-Discovery*. Deerfield Beach, FL: Health Communications, 1988.

Bridges, William. *Transitions: Making Sense of Life's Changes*. Reading, MA: Addison-Wesley, 1980.

Carter, Lanie. *Congratulations! You're Going to Be a Grandmother*. New York: Pocket Books, 1980.

Chamberlain, David. *Babies Remember Birth and Other Extraordinary Scientific Discoveries about the Mind and Personality of Your New-born*. New York: Ballantine, 1990.

Chamberlain, David, and Suzanne Arms. *Babies Know More Than You Think: Exploring the Capacity and Consciousness of New Human Beings* (video). Long Beach, CA: Touch the Future.

Colman, Arthur and Libby. *The Father: Mythology and Changing Roles*. Wilmette, IL: Chiron Publications, 1988.

Elium, Don and Jeanne. *Raising a Son: Parents and the Making of a Healthy Man*. Berkeley, CA: Celestial Arts, 1996.

Gendlin, Eugene T. *Focusing*. New York: Bantam, 1982.

Glennon, Will. *Fathering: Strengthening Connections with Your Children No Matter Where You Are*. Emeryville, CA: Conari Press, 1995.

Greenberg, Martin. *Birth of a Father*. New York: Continuum, 1985.

Griswold, Robert L. *Fatherhood in America: A History*. New York: Basic Books, 1993.

Hendrix, Harville, and Helen Hunt. *Giving the Love That Heals: A Guide for Parents*. New York: Pocket Books, 1997.

Hoffman, Bob. *No One Is to Blame: Getting a Loving Divorce from Mom & Dad*. Palo Alto, CA: Science and Behavior Books, 1979.

Jones, Carl. *From Parent to Child: The Psychic Link*. New York: Warner Books, 1989.

Keen, Sam. *Fire in the Belly: On Being a Man*. New York: Bantam, 1991.

Kirschner, Jan and Tracy. *The Little Goo-Roo: Lessons from Your Baby*. Boulder, CO: Atlas Press, 1997.

Klaus, Marshall, John Kennell, and Phyllis Klaus. *Bonding: Building the Foundation of Secure Attachment and Independence*. Reading, MA: Addison-Wesley, 1996.

Klaus, Marshall and Phyllis. *Your Amazing Newborn.* Cambridge, MA: Perseus Books, 1998.

Kopp, Sheldon. *Raise Your Right Hand against Fear: Extend the Other in Compassion.* Minneapolis, MN: CompCare Publishers, 1988.

Liedloff, Jean. *The Continuum Concept: Allowing Human Nature to Work Successfully.* Reading, MA: Addison-Wesley, 1985.

Lindsay, Jeanne Warren. *Teen Dads: Rights, Responsibilities & Joys.* Buena Park, CA: Morning Glory Press, 1993.

McClure, Vimala. *Infant Massage: A Handbook for Loving Parents,* rev. 3rd ed. New York: Bantam, 2000.

Meade, Michael. *Men and the Water of Life.* San Francisco: Harper, 1997.

Montagu, Ashley. *Life before Birth.* New York: Signet, 1977.

———. *Touching: The Human Significance of the Skin.* New York: Harper & Row, 1972.

Mothering Magazine, eds. *Being a Father: Family, Work, and Self.* Santa Fe, NM: John Muir Publications, 1993.

Olkin, Sylvia Klein. *Positive Parenting Fitness: A Total Approach to Caring for the Physical and Emotional Needs of Your New Family.* Garden City, NY: Avery, 1992.

Osherson, Samuel. *Finding Our Fathers: How a Man's Life Is Shaped by His Relationship with His Father.* New York: Fawcett Columbine, 1986.

Overend, Jenni, and Julie Vivas. *Welcome with Love.* La Jolla, CA: Kane/Miller Books, 1999.

Pearce, Joseph Chilton. *Magical Child: Rediscovering Nature's Plan for Our Children.* New York: Dutton, 1992.

Pollack, William. *Real Boys.* New York: Holt & Company, 1998.

Russell, Marlou. *Adoption Wisdom: A Guide to the Issues and Feelings of Adoption.* Los Angeles: Broken Branch Productions, 1996.

Sears, William. *Becoming a Father: How to Nurture and Enjoy Your Family.* Franklin Park, IL: La Leche League International, 1986.

Smaldino, Carol. *In the Midst of Parenting: A Look at the Real Dramas and Dilemmas*. Port Washington, NY: Brooklyn Girl Books, 2000.

Thevenin, Tine. *The Family Bed: An Age-Old Concept in Childrearing*. Wayne, NJ: Avery, 1987.

Thompson, Keith, ed. *To Be a Man: In Search of the Deep Masculine*. New York: Putnam, 1991.

Verny, Thomas. *Gifts of Our Fathers: Heartfelt Remembrances of Fathers and Grandfathers*. Freedom, CA: The Crossing Press, 1994.

Verrier, Nancy. *The Primal Wound: Understanding the Adopted Child*. Baltimore: Gateway Press, 1993.

Index

About the Author

JACK HEINOWITZ, PH.D., is the father of three children ranging in age from ten to twenty-five. A leading expert in new parenthood and men's issues, he has counseled individuals, couples, and families for more than thirty years. He also presents workshops to expectant and new parents and to health professionals. Based in San Diego, California, where he codirects Parents As Partners Associates with his wife, Ellen Eichler, LCSW, Dr. Heinowitz is the author of the internationally acclaimed *Pregnant Fathers* series.

If you enjoyed *Fathering Right from the Start*, we recommend the following New World Library titles:

Letters to my Son: A Father's Wisdom on Manhood, Life, and Love by Kent Nerburn. This is a powerful collection of beautifully crafted letters on life's toughest questions. Celebrated author Kent Nerburn wrote them to guide his son into adulthood. In this newly revised edition, Nerburn extends his horizons with sections on education and learning, sports and competition, and more. Although written from a father to a son, this eloquent collection carries timeless wisdom for us all.

The Path of Parenting: Twelve Principles to Guide Your Journey by Vimala McClure. *The Path of Parenting* offers twelve principles based on ancient Taoist philosophy and t'ai chi to guide parents in developing long-term philosophical roots as well as short-term solutions about how to be a parent. Filled with practical advice and great inspiration.

The Tao of Motherhood by Vimala McClure. This elegant and inspiring volume adapts the ancient wisdom of Lao Tzu to assist parents with facing the challenges and realizing the joys of raising children.

A Toolbox for Our Daughters: Building Strength, Confidence, and Integrity by Annette Geffert and Diane Brown. From body image to the deadly consequences of unprotected sex, today's teen girls face complex issues their mothers and fathers never dreamed of. Designed as a hands-on tool for parents and daughters as they confront the challenges this transitional period presents, *A Toolbox for Our Daughters* combines experience with an upbeat approach to overcoming problems of teenage girls.

Welcoming Spirit Home: Ancient African Teachings to Celebrate Children and Community by Sobonfu Somé. *Welcoming Spirit Home* focuses on ancestral African wisdom in celebrating community and children. Sobonfu Somé brings to the West the kind of spiritual blessings that she has in her African village by giving examples of how ritual is used in their daily lives. This book includes rituals for healing, conception, after birth, building strong parental bonding, naming children, and coping with miscarriage.

New World Library is dedicated to
publishing books and audiocassettes
that inspire and challenge us to improve the quality
of our lives and our world.

Our books and tapes are available
in bookstores everywhere.
For a catalog of our complete library
of fine books and cassettes, contact:

New World Library
14 Pamaron Way
Novato, CA 94949

Phone: (415) 884-2100
Fax: (415) 884-2199
Or call toll-free (800) 972-6657
Catalog requests: Ext. 50
Ordering: Ext. 52

E-mail: escort@nwlib.com
Web site: www.newworldlibrary.com